57 STATES AND OTHER ANSWERS TO PROJECT 2025

Richard Baxter

To my wife, Julie, my wonderful partner on this wild ride

INTRODUCTION

Finally, after hearing it said every four years, *we actually have an upcoming election that is the most important of our lives.* In fact, it is more important than any since 1860. The good news—thanks to Donald J. Trump—is that the Democratic Party may be on the cusp of a historic victory that will end Trump and Trumpism as a political movement. The paranoid conspiracy theorists will return to the fringe, just as the original America Firsters did after the Second World War. The November election results that I anticipate should marginalize MAGA and narrow the Overton Window sufficiently to remove neo-Jim Crow policy and democratic backsliding from the common discussion. We may well return to the age of Never Again.

Why am I so optimistic under three months from election day? 2024 should continue the favorable post-Trump election results of 2018, 2020, and 2022, the latter of which was refreshed and energized by the Dobbs decision overturning Roe v. Wade. Vice President Kamala Harris, 59 years young, energetic, and experienced, is our standard bearer. The Republican candidate speaks gibberish at rallies and is an adjudicated sexual offender and convicted felon. He is 78 years old, and his age is showing. He has upcoming felony trials in three separate jurisdictions. It is shaping up to be a prosecutor versus convict campaign.

Save for the three-week period after the June 27 debate, the polls have been remarkably close all year. Polls have not been kind to President Biden for most of his presidency, but Democrats won most of the elections. The Harris presidential campaign of 2024 will surely feature many reminders of the dysfunctional

Trump presidency, including January 6th videos, COVID press conferences, and former cabinet members' direct-to-camera ads warning of the consequences of a second Trump term. Trump has not grown his base. He enjoys a high floor and and suffers a low ceiling of support. His modest gains among youths, Latinos, and African American men when he was facing Biden have essentially disappeared.

Who will come to rescue Trump if the polls wane? JD Vance did not bring a wellspring of new support. Their Venn diagram represents two whole circles overlapping each other. Who would vote for one but not the other? Nikki Haley spoke at the Republican convention pursuant to unity after the assassination attempt on Trump, but you won't see much of her going forward. She is popular with independents and moderate Republicans, but she will not work hard for Trump's election. The former South Carolina governor is much more concerned with 2028, and there will be plenty of time to pander to the MAGA base in the meantime. After January 6th and Trump's evident decline in vitality, some past Trump supporters may just stay home. It won't take many former Trump voters' non-votes to move the election in the swing states.

The Democrats are in a very powerful position to keep the White House for the reasons described above and many others. As I write this on August 19, Harris is narrowly ahead in the national polls and Nate Silver gives her a 53.6% chance of winning the Electoral College. Of course, the objective isn't just keeping the White House. It is also keeping the Senate in the face of a very ugly map and picking up the House. The party will need to put its best foot forward to win the trifecta.

Obviously, if the Democrats simply keep the states that they won in 2020, they will handily win the Electoral College 303–235. They could even lose two of the big battlegrounds and still win so long as Pennsylvania isn't one of them. Arizona, Nevada, and Georgia can all go red, and Harris will still win with 270 Electoral College votes (while Trump works feverishly to draft an unfaithful elector). It's more likely that the Democrats pick up two or three large red states. North Carolina, which Trump won by 1.34 points in 2020, Florida (3.36), and Texas (5.58) would all be blue with shifts of just three points as it's a zero-sum game. It helps that North Carolina has a Republican gubernatorial candidate who laments the 19th Amendment giving women the right to vote. Barack Obama won North Carolina and Florida not that long ago. It also helps that Florida has a state constitutional amendment on the ballot this fall, along with an unpopular Republican senator. Texas may be ready to punish Republicans after a hot summer with extended power outages, a governor who pardoned a murderer (and culture war hero), and an oleaginous Ted Cruz up for reelection.

Conventional wisdom tells us that the Republicans will take back the Senate as the map is exceptionally difficult for Team Blue. The Democratic caucus currently holds 51 seats, but West Virginia will surely be lost without Joe Manchin on the ballot. Even if the Democrats pick up all the toss-up states, they will only hold onto the Senate with 50 seats plus the tie-breaking vice president. That's the conventional wisdom. I think the Democrats can do better, but they will need to contest Texas and Florida—two large, expensive states—for the reasons described above. It would be political malpractice to skimp on the necessary resources to win both state's Senate seats. The stakes are very high in 2024, and the Democrats simply cannot afford to phone it in on two winnable states. That doesn't necessarily mean outspending the GOP; it simply means providing ample funds to genuinely compete in both states.

Florida and Texas have uniquely unpopular men in Rick Scott and Ted Cruz, running against solid Democratic contenders Debbie Mucarsel-Powell and Colin Allred, respectively. Team Blue can pick up both seats. That is no small task, as the polls currently show the Republicans winning by mid-single digits, but the margins have been closing, and the races have yet to really begin. The Democratic candidates have served in the House and carry impressive centrist resumes perfect for beating the hard-right MAGA stalwarts who both oppose abortion rights. Ted Cruz has been ritually humiliated by Donald Trump, and Rick Scott long advocated cutting Social Security and Medicare until it was politically untenable. That alone makes him vulnerable in the Sunshine State.

Six years ago, Rick Scott won his Senate seat by about 10,000 votes out of 8.2 million cast. That was a midterm election, which is traditionally viewed as a home field for the GOP. This year, it will be home field for the Democrats—a presidential election—and turnout should be high, especially with Trump on the ballot. Cruz barely survived the very liberal Beto O'Rourke in 2018, winning by just 1.7 points. Allred is a better candidate than Beto, and Texans have had six more years of Ted Cruz. I like our chances, but only if we make it a priority.

Assuming that Democrats win the toss-ups plus Texas and Florida, they will hold 52 seats, a clear majority with a little bit of breathing room. They could still pick up one more this year: Can Lucas Kunce beat Josh Hawley in Missouri? Or they may lose one of the toss-ups. Either way, I am cautiously assuming that the Democrats retain the Senate in 2024.

That leaves the House of Representatives, which currently features an eight-seat advantage for the GOP. Flipping five would win the House for the Democrats. We have seen how fragile their hold is on the speaker's chair through the tribulations of Kevin McCarthy and Mike Johnson. The GOP won 14 congressional districts in 2022 that Biden won in 2020. Every one of these seats is vulnerable. That said, there isn't necessarily an advantage for the party of incumbent presidents that win reelection. President Obama picked up 8 seats, G.W. Bush won 3, while Clinton lost 9. However, Republican governance in the House has been an embarrassment. They have been utterly unable to govern, and that will have consequences at the polls. This book, therefore, assumes that the Democrats will win a 10 to 20 seat majority in the House, at least twice the margin that Nancy Pelosi enjoyed following the 2020 election.

This gives the Democrats the White House, Senate, and House. This book assumes that the Democrats win the White House by comfortably winning the popular vote and the Electoral College, along with narrow majorities in each house of Congress. Will they be able to enact meaningful change with such small congressional margins? Will they be ready to solve many of the problems that have been festering for decades? In a word, yes. The next Congress can be the most productive on record.

The first 100 days are dedicated to systemic changes and enactment of laws that have long been Democratic priorities frustrated by the filibuster. They consist of proposals that received wide Democratic support that can be quickly enacted.

The next 200 days concern items that are new proposals, more complex solutions, or items that will take longer to bring sufficient votes for passage. Since the filibuster will be dead, Congress will not have to wait for perfect bills to meet the 60-vote threshold for enactment. They won't have but one bite at the apple with the next opportunity to come a generation later. This Congress (and those in the future) will be able to improve and expand on bills passed early in the term in addition to addressing complex issues with many moving parts. The system will have become rationalized, making our democracy stronger than ever as it will be more reflective of the will of the electorate. An entrenched minority will no longer be able to hold the nation hostage.

Before we describe the solutions to our problems, it's important to know what we are up against. Read on to learn more about Kevin Roberts, the Heritage Foundation, and Project 2025.

PROJECT 2025

Ultraconservative thought leaders were unhappy with the Trump administration's hapless attempts to remake the American government in their image when they were in power. Trump stumbled frequently as he really didn't understand the government or how it worked. It was nothing like running an inherited, family-owned small business with no other power centers or institutional speedbumps. He surrounded himself with yes-people; if someone didn't show sufficient reverence, they could be gone in a minute.

Trump and "all the best people" he hired didn't know what they were doing. Consequently, they floundered. Republican big money was disappointed in his lack of accomplishments. Granted, he installed three very conservative justices to the Supreme Court with profound implications, and he managed to deliver a massive tax cut to corporations and the wealthy. But that was about it. He built a meager 52 miles of new wall, and Mexico didn't pay for any of it. Few other policy priorities found their way into law, and his feckless COVID response prevented him from doing much else.

The Heritage Foundation is a conservative think tank formed in 1973 by beer magnate Joseph Coors, direct mail pioneer Paul Weyrich, and congressional aide Edwin Feulner. Its founders viewed President Nixon and the Republican Party establishment as too moderate. They were Goldwater supporters, John Birch Society activists, and devout Christians. They resented that the early-'70s GOP was primarily concerned with supporting big business and opposing communism. They felt that cultural issues were getting short shrift and formed the organization to add a conservative cultural vision to the national discussion while still fighting the Reds and advocating tax cuts.

Their connection to the John Birch Society (JBS) is instructive, as the group was on the far right fringe, paranoid, and prone to conspiracy theories. Their founder, Robert Welch, accused President Eisenhower of being a "dedicated, conscious agent" of the communists. They fought the fluoridation of drinking water as a communist conspiracy. They opposed the United Nations, Federal Reserve, and anything that they suspected of fostering a "one world government." They were the original "we're a republic, not a democracy" bunch. William Buckley criticized the group as paranoid and antisemitic and sought to disassociate the conservative movement from the group. While there has always been a dark, paranoid wing of the Republican party, they never really held power until Donald Trump came to town. Several served in the Reagan administration, but their influence was overwhelmed by the GOP establishment. They were still on the outside looking in. Now, they are in the mainstream of the Republican Party. The JBS is welcomed at CPAC conferences, and they fit right in.

The Heritage Foundation gained tremendous influence with Ronald Reagan's election and helped staff his administration as well as the two Presidents Bush. While first opposing Trump as "not conservative," they jumped on the bandwagon as soon as his nomination was apparent. They wasted no time sidling up to the president-elect and played a large role in the transition. They held outsized influence as they conspicuously and ostentatiously supported the new president, while other think tanks remained suspect as some of their leaders were viewed as "Never Trump." The foundation was ranked the number one "Think Tank with the Most Impact on Public Policy" for three years of the Trump administration by the Lauder Institute at the University of Pennsylvania.

In October 2021, the foundation hired Kevin Roberts to run the organization and its affiliated political action committee. Roberts described his role as "institutionalizing Trumpism."

The next year, the foundation began openly supporting

"national conservatism" – a movement fueled by grievance in opposition to modernity, feminism, homosexuality, and the separation of church and state. The group supports traditional families, gender roles, and religion. It is culturally ultraconservative, anti-abortion, and pro-fertility. Importantly, it sees a muscular government role in enforcing its preferred policies.

They are isolationist and skeptical of international organizations, including NATO, the United Nations, the European Union, and the whole alphabet of global institutions established after the Second World War. They do not appreciate the enlightened self-interest of alliances that support Western values, including democracy, free speech, free markets, women's rights, gay rights, pluralism, and a rules-based international order. It's as though no lessons were learned concerning the causes of the two world wars or the success of the Cold War.

Under Kevin Roberts' leadership, the Heritage Foundation changed its position from support to opposition of military aid to Ukraine, claiming that such aid "puts America last." Last year, they established a relationship with the Danube Institute, a Hungarian government-subsidized think tank intended to spread the gospel of national conservatism. Under the ethnonationalist Viktor Orban's leadership, Hungary has become an illiberal democracy employing authoritarian methods of state control. Many on America's far-right – Tucker Carlson, Steve Bannon, and Matt Schalpp, to name a few – have trekked to Budapest to learn the lessons of Orban's Fidesz Party. They want to bring his policies back to the United States.

To that end, Kevin Roberts and the Heritage Foundation have put together Project 2025 – Presidential Transition Project. It is intended to be the roadmap for the next Trump administration. Though Trump is now distancing himself from the proto-authoritarian plans due to their unpopularity, its authors are mostly members of the past Trump administration or one of his campaigns. Like it or not, he is tied at the hip to Kevin Roberts and his troops by virtue of film, photographs, and print, espousing admiration for each other and Project 2025.

Project 2025 lays out its policy goals over 920 pages on four broad fronts: restore the family as the centerpiece of American life, dismantle the administrative state, defend the nation's sovereignty, borders, and bounty against global threats, and secure God-given rights to live freely. That may sound somewhat benign, but in fact, further reading of the plan shows that they are proposing to take our country back to a time when women were second-class citizens and minorities were legally unprotected from discrimination.

They plan to replace career civil servants with political appointees through layers of the federal government in an effort to kill the "deep state." This is contrary to governance in the Western world, where non-political experts in their fields run their departments as directed by the political appointees at the top of the organizational chart. We necessarily do not change personnel from top to bottom with the change of each administration, as we would constantly have "newbies" running the show. Can you imagine any other organization successfully changing out key operating personnel wholesale every four years? How long would the learning curve be after the transition before all departments were competent in their respective domains? Would they ever achieve the competence of departments staffed by career field experts? The vast majority of the bureaucracy is utterly apolitical. We would not be well served in politicizing the staffing, and we would lose continuity in essential and critical departments on a regular basis. The most talented people would avoid such a workplace, further damaging the effectiveness of the government.

They believe in the "unitary executive theory" and would put the entire federal bureaucracy under direct presidential control. The Justice Department, which has essentially been independent since the Watergate era, would routinely take orders directly from the Trump White House.

They plan to completely eliminate the Department of Education and shut down Head Start, the educational program established in 1965 for kids in poverty.

They call for downsizing the National Oceanic and Atmospheric Association for its sins in documenting climate change.

They recommend the largest deportation program in American history and the resumption of "building the wall."

They would cut off support for renewable energy while working to increase coal, gas, and oil production, a catastrophic tradeoff in the face of climate change.

They advocate a return to the gold standard, elimination of the Federal Reserve, and widespread tax cuts. This alone is disqualifying, as no other country in the world backs its currency with gold reserves. No other modern country does without a central bank, and tax cuts would be reckless with $34T debt on the books and growing.

They advocate banning abortion pills and would initially prohibit mailing them by way of the Comstock Act, an 1873 anti-vice law signed by President Ulysses Grant. They assert that abortion is not healthcare, and the Centers for Disease Control and Prevention (CDC) would be prevented from saying otherwise. Medicaid funds would be withheld from Planned Parenthood for *any* healthcare services.

They would ban pornography and imprison those related to its production or distribution. Importantly, they did not define pornography. Teachers and librarians who purveyed in "pornography" would be classified as registered sex offenders. Meanwhile, MAGA World is busy banning books from libraries hither and yon which is why the pornography definition is critical. It is likely that they would write a definition that would effectively criminalize librarians in public schools nationwide. They have regarded nearly any discussion of LGBTQ+ sexuality as pornographic and promoting the lifestyle. They equate being transgender and "transgender ideology" with pornography. Audaciously, the Project 2025 authors want MAGA politicians telling American adults what we can and cannot read or view

The project advocates a wide crackdown on "woke

propaganda," scrubbing the lawbooks and regulations of the terms "reproductive rights," "gender equality," and "sexual orientation." Diversity, equity, and inclusion programs – DEI – would all be shut down. Funding for partners that engage in DEI policy promotion would be cut off. Transgender people would be banned from serving in the military.

They advocate the prohibition of funding for Critical Race Theory training and any data collection regarding race or ethnicity. They do not want data produced that may reveal the disparate impact of policy on minorities.

The Public Service Loan Forgiveness program, which provides student loan relief to borrowers who work in government and non-profit public service jobs, would be shuttered. The Consumer Financial Protection Bureau would also be closed.

The Department of Health and Human Services would be renamed the Department of Life, and a program within it would "maintain a biblically based, social science-reinforced definition of marriage and family."

Kevin Roberts recently said, "We are in the process of the second American Revolution, which will remain bloodless if the left allows it to be." He has a book coming out that was scheduled for a September release but has been postponed to the week *after* the election. Apparently, someone doesn't want the content released in time for voters to evaluate the prose. While Trump tries to claim that he doesn't know Roberts, his running mate, JD Vance, wrote the forward to Roberts' upcoming book. The title was originally "Dawn's Early Light: Burning Down Washington to Save America" but was modified when there was pushback to Roberts' bellicose warning of bloodshed.

From a white Christian nationalist point of view, Project 2025 would be a godsend. If your worldview differs from Trump, Vance, and Roberts, read on for a very compelling alternative vision for the next administration and Congress.

THE FIRST 100 DAYS

KILL THE FILIBUSTER

If either party is going to govern and tackle our mounting problems, the filibuster must go. The filibuster is a Senate rule that was originally intended to ensure that all senators would have their say. No vote could be called until a successful cloture vote ended the debate. Cloture requires a super-majority, currently 60 votes, to allow for a vote. That effectively means minority rule—save for budget reconciliation and presidential appointments—as the majority cannot work its will.

This has practically prevented any meaningful legislation from passing in these polarized times. But it was also a problem in less turbulent eras. "Hillarycare" was killed by 43 Senate Republicans who were, thanks to the filibuster, more powerful than 57 Democrats in 1993. Remember how Mitch McConnell was able to frustrate President Obama's agenda when the Democrats held 59 votes in the senior body? Remember the "Cornhusker kickback" and "Louisiana Purchase" required to get Obamacare to the finish line?

It is unnaturally difficult to pass legislation in our republic as the filibuster is being used in a manner never contemplated by the founding fathers or any other leaders in our first 200 years. The founders intended for Congress to operate through simple majority voting, specifying only a few exceptions for a super-majority requirement. Ratifying treaties, amending the constitution, expelling members of Congress, and post-impeachment conviction in the Senate are the only matters requiring more than a simple majority in the Constitution.

In the past, the filibuster was used to block civil rights

legislation by southern senators. Strom Thurmond, a "Dixiecrat" of South Carolina, holds the record for the longest filibuster when he spoke on the Senate floor for over 24 hours to kill the Civil Rights Act of 1957. President Kennedy proposed civil rights legislation in June of 1963 but failed to overcome a filibuster. It was only after Kennedy was assassinated that President Johnson advanced the legislation and overcame a 72-day filibuster. After the passage of the Civil Rights Act of 1964, the Deep South became solidly Republican. The GOP successfully implemented the "Southern Strategy," and Strom Thurmond switched to the Republican Party in 1964, just two months after the civil rights bill was signed into law.

Kamala Harris has consistently advocated ending the filibuster, which provides political support to the process. However, the president plays no role in ending the filibuster other than advocacy. It is a Senate rule and thus is determined exclusively by the Senate majority. That said, Harris will still be the vice president when the new Senate convenes on January 3rd, and she may need to break a tie to change the rule.

As the use of the filibuster has climbed, there has been talk of modifying the rule. The Senate budget reconciliation process requires only a simple majority and is consequently viewed as a potential way around the filibuster. However, such an approach is frustrated by the "Byrd Rule" that mandates that the process concerns only the budget – essentially taxes and spending. Anything that the Senate parliamentarian finds extraneous to the budget cannot be included in reconciliation. Consequently, killing or liberalizing the Byrd Rule comes up whenever the majority is stymied.

They could eliminate the 60-vote requirement to simply pass a motion to proceed, which would allow debate to begin on a bill while protecting the 60-vote requirement to bring the bill up for a vote. Other suggested changes have included reducing the number from 60% of the Senate to break a filibuster or going old school and requiring that Senators speak from the floor to block the legislation. The problem with this last approach is that it effectively shuts the Senate down from any other business during the filibuster. At present, the body's work continues while the filibustered bill is moved to the sidelines. The problem with the other reforms is that they are far too modest and will bear little fruit.

Harry Reid ended the filibuster for judicial appointments, except the Supreme Court, in 2013 as the GOP was filibustering any and all nominations to the DC Circuit—the second most important court in the country.

Mitch McConnell ended the filibuster for Supreme Court appointments in 2017 as soon as it was convenient and he had the votes.

The filibuster has become a serious problem in our representative democracy. This contributes significantly to America's persistent "wrong track" mood. Gallup has measured "Americans' satisfaction with the way things are going in the U.S." for 45 years. Only briefly has it registered >50% satisfaction in the mid to late 1980s and again in the late 1990s to 2004. The survey has not revealed a satisfaction score of over 46% since January of 2004, over 20 years ago.[1] This roughly corresponds to the spiking of cloture motions filed (attempts to end a filibuster) in 2007 when they doubled to 139 from the previous Congress.

Please note that from 1917 until 1970, there were never more than seven cloture motions filed over a Senate term. The 1970s peaked at 44, the 1980s at 54, and the 1990s at 82. The last Congress (117th) saw 336 cloture motions, just surpassing the preceding Congress, which had 328.[2] For those who prefer governance over chaos, this is a serious crisis, and there is no relief in sight save for killing the anachronistic Senate rule.

The founders gave us a system that requires a simple majority in both houses with a presidential signature to pass legislation. That alone is a high bar. How often are members of one party all on the same page? Senators and representatives have naturally different constituencies and priorities. Rural, suburban, and urban members may be in the same party but not agree on specific legislation. The president may have issues of importance that are not shared by Congress. Getting everyone on the same page to pass legislation is not easy in any event.

We now find ourselves in a place that the founders never intended. There are some politicians—just a few remaining —who genuinely believe the filibuster fosters consensus and moderation. I don't know that it ever did, but it certainly doesn't now. Polls tell us that about 87% of Americans support universal background checks without loopholes to purchase firearms.[3] Even after the Sandy Hook school shooting, where 26 people were slaughtered, including 20 six- and seven-year-olds, the Senate was not able to pass such legislation. The National Rifle Association (NRA) funds many Republican campaigns, it enjoys widespread grassroots support, and it promises GOP candidates well-funded primary opponents if they cross the gun lobby. Consequently, senators who wanted to remain senators simply could not enact a law that enjoyed widespread support. This obstruction would not have been possible without the filibuster. Clearly, consensus-building and moderation didn't stand a chance against radical and powerful interests.

While the Democrats enjoyed a narrow Senate majority the last two terms, Senators Manchin and Sinema opposed killing the filibuster. They will be replaced in 2025 as both seats are up and neither is running for reelection. Republicans had their own holdouts after the 2016 election when the filibuster was useful for Democrats, as the GOP held both houses of Congress and the White House. One of the common warnings against killing the filibuster is that the other party will eventually hold power and wreak havoc without the rule. Does anyone today believe that the Republicans wouldn't eliminate the filibuster if it was convenient and they had the votes?

The filibuster is going away, and good riddance. The only question is, When? It's an anti-democratic rule that has far outlived its original purpose. How many more problems need to stack up before the will of the people can be expressed through their elected leaders? We really are running out of time. While the country is politically polarized, border security and immigration reform can't get to the legislative finish line. MAGA Republicans in Congress openly admit that they do not want to pass any legislation—even their longstanding wish lists—that could be perceived as a Democratic win. We continue to have far higher firearm death rates—murders, accidents, and suicides—than our peers in the developed world. Yet Congress can do nothing. We have $34 trillion of debt, but the parties are sleepwalking into a debt crisis that will not be easily resolved. There is no talk of compromise on our most pressing issues.

The filibuster provides a ready excuse for the failure to execute campaign promises and party platforms. Eliminating the rule will add accountability, which has been conspicuously absent. When one party holds all the levers of power, it will not be able to blame opposition obstruction for its failure to produce. It will need to put up or shut up.

This will be the Democrats' opportunity to do just that. They will prosper in such an environment and enjoy the support of the American people as a functional, responsive government is good policy and will improve people's lives. Perpetual gridlock only serves the interests of nihilists who want to burn down our democratic system. Would-be authoritarians have no better ally than a broken system incapable of governing.

On January 3, 2025, Senate Democrats can end the filibuster with a simple majority vote when they establish Senate rules for the 119th Congress subject to a successful election mandate. This is imperative, as otherwise, our festering problems will only grow even after we win control of all the levers of power.

EXPAND THE SUPREME COURT

C ongress's next act should be expanding the Supreme Court to 13 seats. The Constitution does not set the number of seats; simple legislation does. Membership has varied from five to 10 seats over the years. In this proposal, the Democrats should be prepared in advance to quickly propose and enact the legislation. Furthermore, four candidates for the seats should be vetted and ready to go for the next Congress. In fact, President-elect Harris could unofficially nominate them during the lame-duck period so that Majority Leader Schumer could see that hearings are scheduled for early January so that the nominees are ready for confirmation votes in late January, subject to official nomination and the appropriate legislation.

While court expansion is proposed, a constitutional amendment to establish the size and seating of the body should also be put forward. The Democrats certainly cannot pass the amendment on their own—it will require two-thirds support in each house and ratification by three-quarters of the states—but it may receive Republican support as it will serve their interests.

My proposed amendment is as follows: Set the seats at 13, establish 26-year terms for Supreme Court justices (and newly appointed lesser federal court judges), and provide that one seat is vacated and replaced every two years. New terms would begin in odd-numbered years so that nominations and confirmations would coincide with each new Congress for the Supreme Court's term beginning in October. If nominees were not confirmed in time for the next session of the court, the president could fill the seat without confirmation for two years. Any vacancies would be filled in the same manner—the balance of the respective term with Senate confirmation or two years absent the same.

The 13 post-expansion justices' term ending dates would be based on seniority to establish the rotation. The chief justice position would be the justice with the highest seniority upon a chief justice vacancy after the amendment is ratified. This would de-politicize the position to the extent possible and foster collegiality and consensus building. If there are more than 13 justices at the time of ratification, the most recent appointments would be removed to obtain a membership of 13.

A few items should be added to the constitutional amendment as sweeteners. One would prohibit a president from pardoning themself, removing any question on the subject. Another would modify the power of the pardon such that specific reprieves or pardons would not become effective for 70 days. Either house could overturn the clemency by a simple majority vote within the 70-day period. This would allow review by the current and subsequent congress for pardons issued during the lame-duck session. The pardon power has been abused by many presidents, and none more so than Donald Trump. He often dangled pardons to keep potential witnesses quiet. He pardoned Mike Flynn, George Papadopoulos, Roger Stone, Paul Manafort, and Steve Bannon during the lame-duck period. All five potentially had incriminating testimony or evidence against the president. Perhaps, they would have been more forthcoming with authorities if the president's pardon was subject to the cooperation of Congress. Trump has said he will pardon the January 6th convicts, which encourages more such lawlessness. Bill Clinton had suspect pardons that appeared to help fund his presidential library. Pappa Bush pardoned Casper Weinberger, and Nixon famously pardoned Jimmy Hoffa. The check of Congress should rein in the abuses and perceived abuses that we have seen in the modern era. Non-political pardons for worthy recipients would have nothing to fear, and the purpose of justice would be advanced rather than corrupted.

Federal judges should be prohibited from receiving any gifts exceeding $100 in value from anyone other than immediate family members, who would remain free to be as generous as they like. In years past, conservatives have been troubled as Republican-appointed justices appeared to be less conservative after their appointment. Justices Souter, O'Connor, and Stevens all fall into this category though none more so than Chief Justice Earl Warren (appointed by Eisenhower). The Roe v. Wade decision was rendered by the conservative Burger Court, and the opinion was written by Harry Blackmun—a lifelong Republican. It appears that Leonard Leo and the Federalist Society, among others, have tried to keep the justices close through extraordinary generosity. Though the justices would strongly argue that their vote cannot be bought, generous gifts and invitations to travel and socialize with the super-rich effectively buy influence.

Would conservative justices stray far from their roots if it also meant being shunned by their newfound, wealthy friends who introduced them to such sublime, rarefied air? Consciously? Unconsciously? Maybe, maybe not. We should not even have to ask. It has every appearance of influence-seeking and corruption. It needs to end.

Lastly, I would repeal the 23rd Amendment—a primary sweetener for the GOP—as my next action step would be statehood for Washington, DC, less a small, practically unpopulated federal enclave. In such event, three Electoral College votes would remain to be appointed "in such manner as Congress may direct." Once DC has obtained statehood, the remaining Federal District would not have any permanent residents, and if it did, granting them three Electoral College votes would certainly constitute over-representation. I advocate granting the three votes to the winner of the popular vote until the 23rd Amendment is repealed as called for herein.

While many would complain that the Democrats are

packing the court, I would argue that they are unpacking it. While every current member was nominated and confirmed legally and constitutionally, so too would be the four new justices bringing the justice count to 13. President Obama's nomination of Merrick Garland never received a hearing ostensibly because it came during an election year, yet Amy Coney Barrett was nominated just over a month prior to the 2020 election and was sworn in a week before election day. Both actions cynically broke precedent and would require four new justices to offset their impact.

All the Democratic-appointed members would have been nominated by presidents who enjoyed the mandate of the American people winning both the Electoral College and the popular vote. Half of the current six Republican-appointed members were appointed by Trump, who did not enjoy such a mandate.

The current court also suffers from the appearance of corruption, if not actual corruption. Insurgency flags are flying at the home of Samuel Alito, and Clarence Thomas has taken millions of dollars in gifts and sweetheart real estate deals. Alito, too, has enjoyed generous travel benefits from those who would enjoy his favor. Neil Gorsuch and associates sold a vacation home to the chief executive of a law firm that frequently has business before the Supreme Court.[4] The sale came one month after his court appointment and after the property had floundered on the market for two years. Was the sale timing just a coincidence? Was it just dumb luck having nothing to do with influencing a member of the court? Really? The current court has paved the way to the wholesale reform described herein.

The proposed amendment would be popular among the electorate, even if it could not initially obtain the necessary two-thirds votes in the House and Senate. It would provide political cover for the expansion, and I expect would eventually find the super-majority of votes for passage.

If the constitutional amendment described is enacted, each president serving would appoint two justices per term, or 13% of the court, in an organized and predictable manner. The only exceptions would be filling unforeseen vacancies. Under our current system, Trump filled a third of the court's justices in four years, a one-term volume unseen since Warren Harding a century ago. Even without Machiavellian maneuvering, this is no way to run a railroad.

Our justice system suffers from our highly polarized era. The status quo fuels partisanship. The stakes are incredibly high for each vacancy, whether caused by an untimely death or a justice retiring when a like-minded president can fill their seat. By adding seats, the proportionate impact of each nomination is reduced, and justices won't find it necessary to game their retirement timing. If they pass away or otherwise leave early, their replacement will only fill the balance of their term. It will not be a lifetime appointment, and the stakes of each nomination will be correspondingly reduced.

With 26-year terms for the Supreme Court and newly appointed members of inferior federal courts, administrations will no longer fill seats with the youngest appointees possible to extend the impact of the appointment. The quality of the federal bench will materially improve with 26-year terms rather than the lifetime appointment system that seemed to work well for our first two centuries but not much since.

What happens if the constitutional amendment is not enacted? For the purposes of the next Congress, it doesn't matter. The post-filibuster legislation will accomplish a great deal of desperately needed reform, and the Republicans will not be able to pass legislation to add more seats to the court until they have won all three levers of power—an unlikely event for some time to come. It simply doesn't happen that often.

In the meantime, the court will have been unpacked, and that alone should improve the court's reputation, which has suffered mightily of late. In an APNORC poll in June 2024, only 16% of respondents said they had "a great deal of confidence in the Supreme Court," while 40% indicated "hardly any confidence at all."[5]

For argument's sake, let's assume that the Republicans

take the White House and both houses of Congress in 2028. What then? They could certainly expand the court further while enacting legislation reflecting their priorities. While they would have no reason to add seats to the court in which they already command a 6 to 3 majority, they would certainly eliminate the filibuster and advance conservative legislation. Any suggestion that the Republicans would retain the filibuster out of respect for precedent while holding the votes to kill it have not been paying attention.

Steven Calabresi, a leader of the Federalist Society, the extraordinarily influential conservative group concerned with the courts, has already advocated the wholesale expansion of the federal judiciary. The implications of Supreme Court expansion are not as profound as many conservative pundits and pols will opine. There is no Rubicon to cross. Expansion is wholly lawful and constitutional. It would not be contrary to the wishes or vision of our founding fathers. It would be smart politics and smart policy, potentially ushering in a new era of progress.

STATEHOOD FOR DC: DOUGLASS COMMONWEALTH

With the end of the filibuster, the Democrats will finally be able to give 689,545 Americans taxation *with* representation. While our nation will retain the federal district—the District of Columbia—it will only consist of the White House, Capitol Hill, Supreme Court, National Mall, and contiguous federal parks and properties. Essentially, it will be our seat of government where no one lives.

The balance will become the 51st state.

Cynical Republican arguments notwithstanding, this can be obtained through simple federal legislation. The district approved a statehood referendum in 2016 by a whopping 78%.[6] In 2017 and nearly every term since, the Washington DC Admission Act was introduced in both houses of Congress, where it died under Republican control initially and then due to its inability to obtain 60 votes in Chuck Schumer's Senate.

The same act—slightly modified—can be introduced in 2025. Once modified, passed by the DC Council and both houses of Congress, and signed by the president, we will have a new state. We will have two new Senators appointed by the DC Council (to face the voters in the 2026 general election), and the House representative will receive full member voting status.

The District was created by the District of Columbia Organic Act of 1801 in order to create a permanent federal capitol.

It was comprised of five political units, two obtained from Virginia (that would be ceded back to the state in 1846), and three from Maryland—Washington City, Washington County, and Georgetown. There were only about 14,000 residents at the time, far too small a population for statehood.

They began seeking self-government almost immediately. In 1802, Congress granted the City of Washington a city charter with a locally elected council and a mayor appointed by the president. In 1820, residents were granted the right to elect their mayor. By 1870, largely as a consequence of the Civil War, the district had grown to a population of 131,700.

In the District of Columbia Organic Act of 1871, the three remaining political units were united into one and granted territorial status. They had a bicameral legislature with the president appointing the governor and an 11-member council. Residents elected a council with 22 members. This lasted until 1874, when Congress ended the territorial status after financial calamity, and the president appointed three commissioners to govern the district. This lasted until 1967.

In 1961, by way of the 23rd Amendment to the Constitution, the district was granted Electoral College votes in an amount equivalent to a state (though never more than the least populous state). It was not until the general election of 1964, 90 years after territorial status ended, that district's residents enjoyed any form of democratic representation.

Congress consistently rejected home-rule efforts, and in 1967, President Johnson reorganized the local government into an appointed nine-member council and mayor/commissioner. In 1968, the district was granted the right to elect a board of education and, in 1970, to elect a member of the House of Representatives with non-voting status.

In 1973, Congress approved a limited home-rule that district voters approved in 1974, creating a democratically elected 13-member council and mayor. That system remains in place today.

While the district now enjoys many of the legislative rights of a state, district budgets must be reviewed and enacted by Congress. District legislation is subject to congressional veto. In short, the 689,545 residents of DC not only do not have any voting representation in the House or Senate, they also do not enjoy most of the basic rights that any city does in the 50 states. Absent statehood, Congress could remove DC's limited self-rule at any time through simple legislation.

Washington, DC certainly meets the criteria of a state. It is larger than Vermont and Wyoming and slightly smaller than Delaware, Alaska, and the two Dakotas. Until COVID arrived, DC was growing at a rapid clip. The residents have their own interests, just as any state, and national interests should not govern their administration more than any they do in West Virginia or Alaska.

The taxation without representation argument is a real one. Our nation was founded on the principle of self-governance. It is, therefore, imperative to have the consent of the governed. That residents are taxed at the federal level at the same rate as residents of the 50 states, yet they have utterly no voting representation in Congress, is an abomination. Legally, they have less local control than nearly every city in the country.

If we are that shining city on a hill that Reagan described— a beacon to all the freedom-loving people in the world—how can that be? We cannot consistently advocate democracy all over the world and structurally deny the vote to over a half million people in our own capital.

Some Republicans have argued that the populated portion of the district should simply be returned to Maryland from where it came over 230 years ago. In 1846, they say, DC returned the Virginia portion of its landmass through retrocession, as residents chafed at the lack of benefits and electoral disenfranchisement that came with district citizenship.

That may have made sense in the mid-nineteenth century, but DC's population has long been a discrete political unit, and it does not necessarily share the same interests, ambitions, or priorities as its brothers and sisters in Maryland. Furthermore, Maryland may love its state just as it is without annexing a large political unit that will affect the outcome of statewide elections and the membership of its legislature.

All of our state legislatures except Nebraska are bicameral, which may not be the most efficient way to govern in the modern era. The Douglass Commonwealth would be run by a governor and 13 representatives. The new state will be a high-profile laboratory of democracy, perhaps showing other states the advantages of a streamlined unicameral legislature.

The party of small government should be delighted. Those who advocate that the government closest to the people governs best should also be on board as there will be one government unit running the whole show, and they are very close to the people.

There will not be a reconciliation process between the two legislative houses, which is where mischief and pork are often served together. There will not be overlapping responsibilities of cities, counties, school districts, water boards, and other local districts. There will be one popularly elected body with members of the legislature representing about 53,000 people each.

We will have a new model of streamlined government operating just outside the nation's capital. There is a lot to like in this legislation for good faith actors on both sides of the aisle.

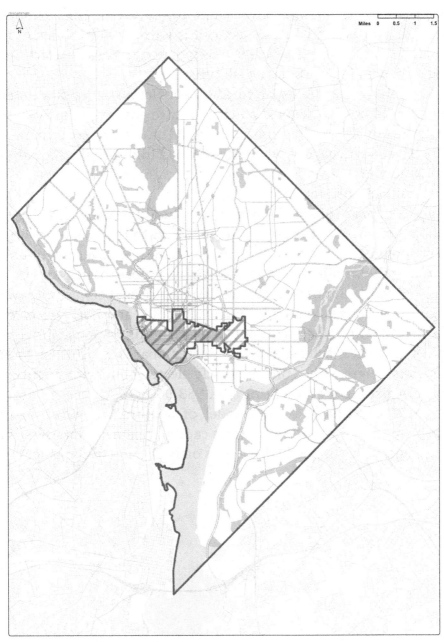

Miles 0 0.5 1 1.5

N

Proposed State of Washington DC

Office of Planning -- October 19, 2016

Government of the District of Columbia

This map was created for planning purposes
from a variety of sources. It is neither a
survey nor a legal document. Information
provided by other agencies should be
verified with them where appropriate.

THE VOTING RIGHTS ACT OF 2025

The original Voting Rights Act was passed in 1965 and subsequently updated and amended five times from 1970 to 2006. After its hard-fought, bipartisan passage in 1965, successive updates and extensions would routinely glide through Congress. In 2006, the House approved the Voting Rights Act (390-33), and the Senate passed it unanimously (98–0) without amendment. The original Voting Rights Act of 1965 was still doing its job, and both parties publicly supported its periodic updates and extensions.

In 2013, everything changed when the Supreme Court struck down the Voting Rights Act's coverage formula for the determination of jurisdictional applicability in Shelby County v. Holder. The original Voting Rights Act outlawed racial and ethnic discrimination in our electoral process. It gave teeth to our constitutional rights provided in the 14th and 15th Amendments. Importantly, it recognized jurisdictions with a history of egregious discrimination. Special rules would apply to those jurisdictions, which would need to get Justice Department approval, known as preclearance, before they could change laws or rules concerning elections.

In 2013, Chief Justice Roberts wrote the majority opinion that the Voting Rights Act's coverage formula was outdated and unreasonably burdensome for subject jurisdictions that did not include a documented recent history of discrimination. In her dissent, Justice Ginsburg noted that "throwing out preclearance when it has worked and is continuing to work to stop discriminatory changes is like throwing away your umbrella in a rainstorm because you are not getting wet." The following decade has proved Ginsburg right, as myriad voting laws and rules were enacted that had the intention and effect of suppressing the votes of minorities and others that tended to vote Democratic.

Justice Roberts' opinion essentially tasked Congress with prescribing a new coverage formula that could be justified by current circumstances. With the protection of the Shelby County opinion, Republicans stopped cooperating in any meaningful reform to the Voting Rights Act. The Senate filibuster rule gave them the power to kill any legislation that would resurrect any form of preclearance. They are satisfied with leaving the rules unenforceable. In red states, the GOP is actively suppressing the vote if not for naked racism but because minorities tend to vote Democratic.

When the preclearance section of the Voting Rights Act was killed, the GOP got busy making mischief in myriad ways. They moved polling places further from college campuses and public transportation stops while understaffing the voting operations. We often see long lines of students and minorities voting on election day, while older white folk are usually able to quickly vote without lines or in short lines a few miles away in the suburbs. In Georgia, they added insult to injury. They have notoriously long voter lines in minority areas, and now it is a crime to provide food or water to those standing in line. With its capital city nicknamed "Hotlanta," standing in line outside can be uncomfortable. Instead of setting out to rid the system of lines and improve the ease of voting, the Georgia legislature took the time to criminalize the watering and feeding of patient voters.

In a practice known as "voter caging," activists will mail letters to registered voters who are likely to support Democrats just past the registration deadline. They create a list of the mail returned undelivered and then challenge those voters due to improper address after it's too late for the voter to cure their registration. They frustrate the voting rights of college students as they tend to move a lot and do not necessarily update their registration when they move from one dorm room to another. They also tend to vote Democratic. In the 1980s, the Republican Party would send such mail to predominately African American addresses and challenge the returns. They were caught, and it was a violation of the Voting Rights Act. Ultimately, they entered into a consent decree to cease such activity.[7] The consent decree expired in 2017. However, voter caging didn't end. It was just farmed out to like-minded, "independent" operations.

Several red states have recently required proof of citizenship for voter registration, which can be modestly difficult and expensive to obtain. However, the same information can be easily cross-checked through government databases without the necessity of snail mail and a civilian working their way around multiple bureaucracies to obtain and provide a certified birth certificate. Unless there is genuine difficulty determining a voter's citizenship, why require them to bring a physical copy of their birth certificate to register to vote? Many Americans do not have their birth certificate, and obtaining the same may be time-consuming and will certainly be a hassle. What office has the original document, and how much will it cost to obtain? Election officials can answer this and quickly confirm the information online. They are professionals and this is in their wheelhouse. Why put voters through an unnecessary process? It's just one more bad-faith tripwire introduced quickly after the preclearance requirement was removed. It is intended to suppress the vote of minorities and young people.

Prior to the 2000 election, Florida purged 58,000 voters from the rolls ostensibly due to felony convictions or death.[8] Florida was one of eight states that prohibited ex-felons from voting unless restoration of voting rights was specifically requested and received—an infrequent occurrence. A private firm compiled the purge list and made a lot of errors. People were removed from the rolls that merely had past misdemeanor convictions or had similar names to ex-felons or deceased people. The flawed nature of the list was discovered well before the general election, but the Secretary of State's office chose not to act. Many legally registered voters showed up to exercise their franchise and were turned away. They could not vote in the 2000 election. African Americans make up 11% of the Florida electorate but represent 44% of the faulty voter purge list. Using stricter purge criteria, it was determined that approximately 12,000 voters were erroneously removed as felons. The U.S. Commission on Civil Rights extrapolated that 4,752 Gore voters were unable to vote—nine times the 537 votes that determined the Florida election. It was determinative. There were many other problems in Florida—faulty old machines in minority areas with far higher "spoilage" rates—ballots cast that could not be counted, long lines, and voters in line erroneously turned away at poll closing. The election administration was largely absent, unable to help voters that had been disenfranchised in real-time, among other things. The Republican Party learned an important lesson in that election —there are many ways, large and small, to give their candidates a leg up when running an election. That was 24 years ago, and they have not slowed up. It has only gotten worse.

In Alabama, they added the voter ID requirement shortly after preclearance was overturned. Then, they closed nearly half of the Driver License offices in the state—the office where one obtains the required state-issued identification—and surprise, surprise, most of the closed offices were in areas that served majority African American areas.[9] Texas passed laws severely punishing ineligible voters who vote. One African American woman received a five-year sentence for submitting a provisional ballot while on supervised release for a federal felony tax conviction.[10] She did not know this made her ineligible to vote in Texas (it shouldn't), and it took six years for her conviction to be overturned. Given the ability to introduce unnecessary obstacles to minority voter participation, many red states acted fast and put protocols in place that will last for years before the courts can overturn them.

New voter ID laws have been the most insidious form of voter suppression. On its face, it seems reasonable to simply say that voters should have identification—you need ID to get on a plane, cash a check, or buy beer, right? However, the new laws tend to be very strict and inflexible. Someone who is registered as John Doe with a current state-issued driver's license reading Jonathan Doe would not be eligible in many states. In Texas, a woman who changes her name after marriage or divorce needs to promptly change her ID and voter registration so that they are identical. If a middle initial appears on one document, it must appear on the other. Are these good-faith requirements intended to "true the vote" or technicalities that can be used to bar some voters while giving a pass to others?

It's very important to remember that voter impersonation is extraordinarily rare. There are precious few documented cases. Have you ever gone to vote and been turned away as someone already voted in your place? Of course not. Our biggest problem with voters is getting them to show up and vote once, and there is no evidence of any multiple or non-citizen voting on any scale. If the genuine purpose of a voter ID law is to make sure the voter is the same individual who registered, this can be easily accomplished without Draconian laws filled with superfluous barriers.

The Transportation Security Administration (TSA) has more than a dozen approved forms of identification to use in screening. The airlines are not interested in preventing you from flying on a technicality—they want you to fly. That is the business they are in. Fun fact: If you do not have any ID, you can still board an airplane. The TSA makes allowances, and they have an identification verification process. They will simply interview you and confirm your identity otherwise. There are many verification resources online. It is only if you fail to cooperate with the verification process or they cannot find you in any relevant database that you cannot fly. The very same approach should be used in the voter registration and voting processes. We need to operate exclusively in good faith and reject any approaches of culling the voter rolls for partisan advantage. That is throwing the baby out with the bathwater. We are a democracy. We need to reflect the will of all of the people and obtain the consent of the governed. Preventing American citizens from exercising their franchise is extraordinarily cynical and corrupt. Such practices should not be acceptable to anyone who supports self-government and our American way of life.

In 2021, the Freedom to Vote Act was introduced in the Senate. The companion John R. Lewis Voting Rights Advancement Act was presented in the House. Between the two, new preclearance criteria would be implemented that pass the Supreme Court's Shelby County test. Automatic and same-day voter registration, voting by mail, and early voting periods would be established for federal elections. Election Day would be a federal holiday. Voter roll purges would be held to new standards, preventing current practices that erroneously remove legitimate (disproportionately minority) voters. Corruptly interfering with voter registration and voting would be criminalized. Election security—post-election audits, etc.—would be established, as would criteria for redistricting in an effort to minimize gerrymandering. Campaign finance would also be addressed, including a prohibition of dark money.

This should be the next priority in Congress in the new filibuster-free era. Both bills should be reintroduced, including the following updates:

Public financing for House of Representatives races. I would replace Klobuchar's small donor matching protocol with a robust, federally funded House campaign funding system through the use of matching funds. In 2022, the average House winner spent $2.79 million, and the average loser spent $804,000.[11] It would cost about $3 billion every two years to fund every district with $7 million (2.5 times last cycle's average winner). Using $3 billion to mitigate big money and special interests in a $6.5 trillion budget is dirt cheap. It is an extraordinarily modest cost in the scheme of things. This is the foundation of our representative democracy.

Participation would necessarily be voluntary. Candidates could continue to fund their campaigns under the current system. However, public funding would be a very attractive alternative. Match small donors (up to $250) on a 10-to-1 basis. Prohibit participants from receiving funds from anyone other than individual citizens. Accept generous spending limits that may be raised if a general election opponent is not participating in public financing and is exceeding the public financing spending limits.

Currently, members of Congress are expected to spend about 50% of their time fundraising and even more in election years. Public financing would allow candidates and elected officials to spend their time meeting voters and legislating rather than courting prospective paymasters.

Require ranked choice voting (RCV) or top two primaries (also known as jungle primaries) in Senate and House elections. At various times, both parties have opposed these voting methods as they may reduce the power of political parties. However, when such proposals face the voters, they often win. RCV and blanket primaries both reduce the power of the extremes to the benefit of the whole electorate. In our highly polarized era, this is just what the doctor ordered.

A top two primary puts all the candidates on one primary ballot, and the winners of the top two spots proceed to the general election irrespective of their political party. This will mean that Republicans will face Republicans and Democrats face Democrats in many House races where 84% of the seats are safe. Of course, most races will still be between Republicans and Democrats, but the candidates will need to respect the whole electorate rather than just party activists. A member of Congress in a safe district will need to worry about potential challengers from the same party in the general election. It will no longer make sense to cater exclusively to their base. A moderate member of their party could provide a greater threat, as they could unite the moderates in their party with the other party. This dynamic does not currently exist in over 40 states. This protocol is successful even if challengers do not beat the incumbent, as it forces members to respect all the voters.

RCV comes in many forms. I advocate a nonpartisan primary where the top three to five candidates make the general election, irrespective of party. In the general election, voters will rank the candidates. In the first round, a candidate who gets a majority of first-choice votes wins. If no one gets a majority, then the last-place finisher is eliminated, and their second-choice preferences are counted as first-preference votes in the second round. This continues until one candidate has obtained a majority of votes (50%+1).

In most states, our current voting system features first-past-the-post (FPTP) races wherein the person who gets the most votes wins, even if the total is well short of a majority. When combined with our partisan primary system, it means that the winning candidate is typically beholden primarily to their party activists. *The Cook Political Report* identifies 69 competitive House races in 2024, which is just under 16% of the body.[12] Of these 69, 22 are rated toss-up seats, meaning that only 5% of House districts are not leaning one way or the other. It's likely that Politburo seats were more competitive.

That is how we end up with representatives such as Matt Gaetz and Marjorie Taylor Greene, who spend much of their time trolling the Democrats and bitterly opposing Republicans who dare to work across the aisle. They are beholden only to their party base. They do not need to worry about Democrats or independents in their safe seats. They need to be concerned about being primaried by a Republican on their right flank. Team Blue also has safe seats where the interests of the GOP and the center-right need not be considered. Top two primaries and RCV solve that problem.

If Gaetz and Greene's elections were conducted with a top two primary, they would need to worry about a Republican opponent who made it to the general election. A deep red district may well end up with a far-right Republican against a center-right Republican, which gives the voters a real choice compared to the status quo. In their districts, only a Republican will knock them off. How would they act in office if they potentially faced a good government, right-center Republican opponent every two years? Or a principled, libertarian-leaning Republican? It would change everything. Out of necessity, they would work across the aisle, and they would find more willing partners on the other side. If they couldn't manage that, they would probably not survive too many election cycles.

RCV also encourages consensus and prevents candidates from ignoring the interests of a large minority of the district. Alaska passed RCV by referendum and shortly thereafter elected Mary Peltola, a Democrat, to represent the state in the House of Representatives. She beat Sarah Palin, a Republican, who had received a clear plurality of the vote. In an FTPT system, the race would be over, and the highly polarizing culture warrior would be representing the statewide district. Instead, Peltola kept her head down and campaigned as a problem solver—a workhorse—and that appealed to most of the electorate. She will need to govern the same way, or she will lose her seat in a state that leans heavily Republican.

There is now a Republican-supported attempt to repeal Alaska's RCV law by referendum in the November election. In fact, the GOP is actively trying to preempt the adoption of RCV systems nationwide. The party, now under the full control of the MAGA crowd, is nihilistic and opposes anything that might threaten far-right members in safe red seats. They thrive on the current polarization and are working hard to grow it. We need a federal law that mandates top two primaries or RCV election systems (states would get to choose their preference) in federal elections. It will be a major strike against extremism and will frustrate proto-authoritarian attempts to divide us further still.

The passage of an updated Voting Rights Act is imperative if we want our government to reflect the will of the people. Under our current system, a powerful minority is attempting to game the system to maintain a position of privilege. Voter suppression takes many forms, all of which can be taken down or mitigated in 2025.

ENSURE ABORTION RIGHTS NATIONWIDE

N ow that the first four priorities have been achieved —all intended to foster democracy and make Washington work again—it is time to enact high-priority policies. Reproductive rights are at the top of the list.

The Women's Health Protection Act of 2023 was introduced last year after the Dobbs decision in 2022. It essentially codifies Roe v. Wade by way of federal legislation. It prevents states from restricting abortion services prior to fetal viability. Here is the summary of the bill from the congressional website:[13]

This bill prohibits governmental restrictions on the provision of and access to abortion services.

Before fetal viability, governments may not restrict providers from

- using particular abortion procedures or drugs,
- offering abortion services via telemedicine, or
- immediately providing abortion services if delaying risks the patient's health.

Furthermore, governments may not require providers to

- perform unnecessary medical procedures,
- provide medically inaccurate information, or
- comply with credentialing or other conditions that do not apply to providers who offer medically comparable services to abortions.

Additionally, governments may not require patients to make medically unnecessary in-person visits before receiving abortion services or disclose their reasons for obtaining services.

After fetal viability, governments may not restrict providers from performing abortions when necessary to protect a patient's life and health. The same provisions that apply to abortions before viability also apply to necessary abortions after viability.

Additionally, states may authorize post-viability abortions in circumstances beyond those that the bill considers necessary.

Further, the bill recognizes an individual's right to interstate travel, including for abortion services.

The bill also prohibits governments from implementing measures that are similar to those restricted by the bill or that otherwise single out and impede access to abortion services unless the measure significantly advances the safety of abortion services or the health of patients and cannot be achieved through less restrictive means.

The Department of Justice, individuals, or providers may sue states or government officials to enforce this bill, regardless of certain immunity that would otherwise apply.

Intractable opposition to abortion rights in the early days post Roe v. Wade came in part due to the actual process of changing the law. Unlike our European and Canadian peers, abortion became legal in the United States when the Supreme Court ruled that it was constitutionally protected prior to fetal viability based on a penumbra of rights found in the Constitution, including the right to privacy. The voters had no say in the decision. Most legislatures had laws on the books prohibiting abortion, and just like that, they were all overturned. It did not seem fair to about a third of our electorate, many of whom were following their deeply held religious beliefs.

By the 1980s, nearly all Europeans and Canadians enjoyed abortion rights within the first 12 to 24 weeks of pregnancy. With exceptions, this was obtained through the legislative process. European abortion opponents could take comfort in the fact that they could change the laws if they could rally sufficient support at the polls. American opponents of abortion could not find such comfort. Instead, they became enraged, embittered, and probably the strongest contingent of single-issue voters in the country.

Now, in the post-Dobbs world, abortion opponents can take such comfort. They won by overturning Roe v. Wade, but they have subsequently lost a lot of elections and are just now beginning to realize how popular abortion rights are in the United States. While Roe had been a major catalyst in the formation of the modern conservative movement, Dobbs is helping to kill that same movement. The center now belongs to the Democrats and should so long as abortion rights remain an issue.

So, if the Democrats do the right thing and protect abortion rights prior to fetal viability nationwide, will they stop winning all those elections? Probably not. As stated before, good policy is good politics. Abortion opponents will not go away, and the issue has moved to the legislative branch. Pro-choice Americans will not be lulled again into thinking they have a constitutional right that is unassailable at the ballot box. Abortion will be an issue, large or small, in every election in the foreseeable future. Fortunately, the Democrats are on the right side of the question. It is important that they enact the Women's Health Protection Act early in the next Congress.

RAISE THE MINIMUM WAGE

T hanks to significant wage increases during the COVID pandemic, this issue is less pressing than it has been in the past. Nonetheless, this victory must be consolidated, and the Democrats must pass a material increase in the national minimum wage with annual **cost-of-living adjustment** (COLA) increases to keep pace with inflation. I support the Raise the Wage Act of 2023 (S.2488) introduced by Senator Sanders last year. It would phase in an increase to $17/hour over six years.

It is hard to believe that just a few years ago many a head of household was making $7.25/hour or $15,080 a year if working a 40-hour week, 52 weeks a year (no vacation or sick days). It's even harder to believe that this is still the federal minimum wage. Can you imagine a couple with two kids, both working full-time and earning the minimum wage? What would their life be like bringing in a whopping $2,500/month combined before taxes? What would their kids' life be like? What kind of future would they all face?

Last year, the Center for American Progress found that nearly 40 million workers—about one in four—would directly benefit from an increase in the minimum wage to $15/hour. Further, it would significantly narrow the gender and ethnic wage gaps faced by women, Latinos, and African Americans.[14]

It's been 15 years since the last time the minimum wage was raised in July 2009. The purchasing power of $7.25 has been eroded by 45.84%. The 1979 minimum wage of $2.90/

hour would be $13.34 through May 2024 if it had kept up with inflation, never mind the productivity gains. The Economic Policy Institute reports that from 1948 to 1979, productivity increased 2.5% per annum while wages nearly kept pace at 2.4% per year. However, from 1979 to 2022, productivity increased by 64.7%, yet real wages only increased by 14.8% in the same period. If the minimum wage kept up with inflation and productivity increases since 1979, the minimum wage would be $21.97 today—more than triple the actual minimum wage.[15]

The age-old arguments against a minimum wage increase are that it will cost jobs, add to inflation, hurt low-skilled workers, and won't do much to reduce poverty anyway.[16] So says the CATO Institute, a libertarian think tank that opposes both an increase in the minimum wage and, traditionally, the entire concept of a minimum wage.

The issue of job loss is less relevant with a 4.3% unemployment rate and relatively low unemployment over the last decade, except during the COVID pandemic. Will more pizza joints lay off their delivery drivers and use Uber Eats? Will fast-food restaurants install more order kiosks to reduce the number of cashiers? Yes and yes. In fact, that trend is in place without an increase in the national minimum wage. Nonetheless, our very strong and resilient job growth will absorb any wage increase, job losses, and then some. There are more jobs than workers across the country.

Will the increase reignite inflation? No. While increases in wages will put pressure on restaurant food prices, remember that labor costs are about 31% of sales in the business.[17] Not all payroll consists of minimum wage staff, and the increases would be phased in over six years. The system will efficiently absorb higher wages for the lowest-paid workers.

What would be the impact on the lowest skilled workers with a higher minimum wage? All things being equal, they would be the first to go in the event of layoffs. They would also be hired only after more skilled workers were unavailable at the same wage. That said, minimum wage employers will still need staff, and since they are paying minimum wage, the lowest skilled workers will be the lion's share of their applicants. The low-skilled workers—those just obtaining employment for the first time or returning to the labor rolls after a change of circumstances—will still need to be trained by their new employer. While they will be the last hired, corresponding to their skill set, they will still be hired in an economy with 3% - 5% unemployment and an aging population that is reducing the worker participation rate.

The most specious argument is that it does little to reduce poverty. The previous hikes were much smaller as less time elapsed between increases to the minimum wage. A material increase that takes workers above the poverty line and builds in COLA will all but eliminate poverty among the employed. Our current system allows full-time workers to toil in poverty and collect government assistance. Once workers are assured of a livable wage, a primary cause of poverty will be reduced, and more attention can be dedicated to the remaining causes.

There are two key beneficiaries of effectively doubling the minimum wage. First, the workers and their families. Their lives will be materially better across the board—habitation, transportation, food, clothing, and time with family—time to nurture and instill values, time to recharge, and time to be together.

The other beneficiary is the U.S. taxpayer. Families that earn $70,000 in wages do not need SNAP, WIC, or general assistance. Single parents with two kids working full time will earn about $35,000 per year—about 140% of the poverty rate at $17/hour.

The system is not working if full-time minimum wage employees are necessarily eligible for the entire alphabet of assistance programs. Full-time work should provide a living wage that does not require government assistance. The taxpayer should not effectively subsidize minimum wage employers.

This should be early on the Democrats' agenda for the next Congress, and it should not be controversial.

THE NEXT 200 DAYS

ENACT COMPREHENSIVE IMMIGRATION REFORM

In January, the GOP missed an opportunity to pass an immigration reform bill that answered nearly all of their priorities—except for pleasing Donald Trump. It also exposed their cynicism. The Republican Party wants to have the political issue a lot more than they want the problem solved. The GOP base is serious about wanting a secure border. Big-money Republican donors prefer to have cheap labor that can be exploited. The Republicans have now sabotaged the most conservative border security bill in memory at the demand of the former president. In 2025, the Democrats will have an opportunity to solve this problem on Democratic terms. In so doing, they may well please 80% of the electorate.

In 2013, the Senate passed S.744—the Border Security, Economic Opportunity, and Immigration Modernization Act 68-32. John Boehner was not able to bring this bill up in the House as it failed the Hastert Rule—it did not have the majority support of the majority (Republican) party. It would have easily passed the House with bipartisan support, but it also would have cost Boehner his job. I suspect that he regrets not bringing the bill up and retiring two years earlier, having performed a courageous duty for the country. History would have been kind. Just imagine what our country would be like had the bill been enacted in 2013. Donald Trump's rallying cry in 2016 was "Build the wall." Absent that tentpole issue, where would his campaign have been? Would it have had as much energy? Would it have gotten all those traditional non-voters off their sofas in the industrial heartland? We will never know.

The Democrats need to use the 2013 bill as the foundation of comprehensive immigration reform in 2025. Resources will be provided to genuinely secure the border and quickly adjudicate asylum claims. E-Verify will be incorporated throughout the country so that only those here lawfully will be able to work. Following the 2013 bill's pattern, undocumented workers here continuously since at least December 31, 2023, would be able to legally stay, subject to registration as provisional immigrants, a clear background check, a clean criminal record, and payment of fees, fines, and back taxes. Means-tested public assistance would not be available to provisional immigrants. There would be a path to citizenship so that we do not create a cohort of second-class citizens who are never able to fully participate in the community.

Those who do not have clean criminal records will need to promptly return to their countries of citizenship. The border will need to be physically secured, and our legal and employment systems will need to catch any unlawful newcomers and prevent those who slipped through from remaining in the country. This component of the great compromise that provides "amnesty" and a path to citizenship must be upheld.

Our citizens and lawful residents should not have to compete with undocumented workers for jobs. The pay for manual labor and other services that the undocumented have traditionally performed will materially increase. The lives of the least of us will significantly improve, which will make us a greater country per se.

The 2013 bill required certain border security benchmarks —triggers—to be achieved before any privileges would be granted to registered provisional immigrants (RPIs). The Republicans were wary of granting "amnesty" without corresponding improvements to border security, which they claim was the downfall of President Reagan's 1986 immigration reform. Not only must additional, reinforced border security be in place before the RPI phase, but the bill essentially doubled the number of border patrol officers to 38,405 and dedicated $46.3 billion to border security.

Additional required triggers include 700 miles of new fencing or walls fully constructed and in place, new watchtowers, ground sensors, mobile surveillance systems, portable contraband detectors, radiation isotope identification devices, radar systems, marine vessels, helicopters, and unmanned aircraft. The bill requires 24-hour surveillance of the border using many smart technology tools. Practically speaking, any genuine concerns over security are addressed in the 2013 bill and should be included in the 2025 legislation.

The 2013 bill would need to be updated to provide for quickly processing asylum claims, which would include hiring immigration judges and court personnel and providing temporary housing for the claimants. We need to flood the zone. This would put an end to the widely criticized "catch and release" system where asylum applicants are allowed in the country pending the adjudication of their asylum claims. Once the resources are surged to this end, the number of applicants should materially decrease as the vast majority do not legally meet the criteria for asylum status. They are primarily economic refugees coming from poor, crime-ridden countries seeking a better life for their families. That is not grounds for asylum. They will need to operate legally within our immigration system or go elsewhere.

The 2013 bill was genuinely comprehensive, addressing border security, internal enforcement, undocumented individuals currently in the country, and the immigration system going forward. The bill added merit-based immigration, where applicants are graded on a point system for their ability to contribute to the United States. Science, technology, engineering, and math (STEM) graduates with secured employment would receive work visas ("green cards"). The H1B visa program for highly skilled workers would be extended with restrictions to prevent abuse. An INVEST visa would be created for investors and entrepreneurs who were starting new businesses. Our nation is richer for every doctor, engineer, and entrepreneur we have.

The world is a very competitive place, and it is only growing more so. We are not graduating enough computer scientists and engineers to maintain a qualitative edge in technology. We need to import the best and brightest while we are still the top destination for the same. Absent such an effort, our international competitors will benefit from the talent that will ignite and support future technological advancement and economic growth. It would accelerate the decline of our competitive advantage, and we would have no one to blame but ourselves.

The 2013 bill discontinued the diversity lottery to make room for the new pathways to legal residency. The DREAM Act would be codified, finally creating legal residency for undocumented individuals brought into the country as minors. A "W" visa would be created for low-skilled, non-agricultural workers, with a volume that could be adjusted based on our workforce needs. Green cards would no longer be allocated on a per-country basis, which would help reduce the existing backlog of applications.

The non-partisan Congressional Budget Office (CBO) estimated that the 2013 bill would reduce the federal deficit by $197 billion over the first 10 years and $690 billion over the next 10 years.[18] The Social Security Administration estimated that it would increase revenues by $260 billion over the first 10 years while costing only $23 billion.[19] Immigration is, in fact, an economic juggernaut that has created much of the prosperity that we enjoy today. It will contribute even more if we elevate our game in expanding the legal spots and filling them with applicants who can contribute right away.

Lastly, it will take an issue off the table that has been divisive and contributed to our growing polarization over the past 20 years. The Democrats need to burnish their credentials as problem solvers, and putting this issue to bed will do just that.

ENACT COMPREHENSIVE GUN SAFETY REFORM

We need comprehensive gun safety reforms that will materially and undeniably make our nation safer. It is important that we go big and modernize the rules governing firearms, and we need to do it entirely consistent with the 2nd Amendment as found in precedent, including the very consequential Heller decision.

The good news is that the 2nd Amendment is not our enemy. We need to make sure that voters know that Democrats fully support the amendment as written, as intended, and as interpreted over the past 234 years. We can solve our gun problem entirely within the bounds of our Constitution. That won't prevent passionate opposition from claiming otherwise, which is why it is important that we avoid half-measures. We don't just need to win the argument—we need to demonstrate post-passage that our firearm laws work and that no law-abiding citizen is unduly burdened in the process. We don't need piecemeal legislation that can be slow-walked and blocked in bad-faith negotiations.

We need a bill that is so effective and consequential that legislators will take that tough vote even with the knowledge that it may be politically painful in 2026. In short, the gun safety bill needs to be extraordinary.

In several instances, I have suggested previous legislation

as the foundation of a law to be enacted in 2025. There really isn't one on this subject—none that meets the test of being extraordinary and comprehensive. There are several smaller bills that can be incorporated into a comprehensive bill. Polls tell us that universal background checks and other common-sense reforms are politically popular—80/20 issues—however, the 20% in opposition can be rather passionate and paranoid. The reforms need to be passed in one comprehensive bill rather than piecemeal, as the gun lobby remains very powerful and has sympathetic lawmakers on both sides of the aisle. It will be a tough vote for many and should not be wasted. We need to enact the whole gamut of reform, as it may be a long time until we have control of all three houses again. I propose the following:

Universal background checks. These checks are for firearms and ammunition purchases and/or transfers without exception. If a gun is being transferred to anyone, even a family member, the sale must be documented and approved through the federal background check system. Any federal firearm licensed (FFL) gun dealer will be required to provide background checks during regular business hours for a set fee that makes it worth their while. The sale will then be documented, and begin to build a federal database of lawful gun owners, guns, and ammunition.

Mandatory waiting period. A nationwide minimum 10-day waiting period for the delivery of purchased firearms.

Civil liability for firearms safety. Establish strict civil liability for property damage, injury, or death caused by the usage of firearms or ammunition and provide for federal courts to adjudicate claims. The stated purpose of the 2nd Amendment is to provide for a "well-regulated Militia," and we can all agree that members of the same would suffer penalties for losing their firearms or storing them in a haphazard manner. Just as we are responsible for our negligence on our property or while driving, we should be responsible for securing our firearms and ammunition and subject to civil liability if they damage others through irresponsible or criminal use.

The only safe harbor for a gun owned or purchased after the law is enacted would be its voluntary registration or a subsequent sale with a successful, documented background check. Reporting the loss or theft of firearms and/or ammunition to police in a timely manner could mitigate a gun owner's relative negligence, but it would not provide safe harbor. Ultimately, gun owners would need to treat the objects like deadly weapons, and ownership would include the legal responsibility to keep firearms and ammunition secure.

Require liability insurance to purchase a firearm. Financial hardship waivers would be provided to those without sufficient income or assets to afford insurance for three guns or less. Additionally, evidence of financial responsibility could be provided in lieu of the required insurance. A minimum coverage of $1 million would be required with an annual COLA. Required insurance would cover accidents and negligence that create liability to third parties. It would not cover the intentional acts of the insured, as that is not how insurance traditionally operates.

Among other things, such coverage would create a moral hazard. The insurance industry cannot be upended by a new underwriting standard if we are to maintain an efficient and reliable insurance system with wide and deep coverage. Private insurance companies will welcome the new business as described, and our insurance marketplace should make rates relatively inexpensive, thus not unduly burdensome. Those without a history of criminality, negligence, or large firearms caches should be able to get firearms liability added to their homeowner's insurance policy by a cheap, simple rider. Those with a sketchy history or a sizeable inventory of guns may find the insurance to be expensive and consequently decide to forgo the purchase of an additional firearm. The insurance underwriters' job is to determine and price risk. Adding this element to the purchase process will add financial accountability to ownership of deadly weapons and encourage best practices in the purchase, possession, and sale of firearms.

Establish a federal gun owner, gun, and ammunition

database. All sales and transfers require registration, which will be established through the background check process. Otherwise, registration of existing firearms is voluntary, though encouraged by the reduced liability that it would provide.

Repeal the 2005 Protection of Lawful Commerce in Arms Act (PLCAA) that provides unique immunity to gun manufacturers and dealers. Allow for federal courts to adjudicate firearms industry civil claims.

Repeal any Tiahrt amendments still in effect. The amendments, named after their original House sponsor, frustrate law enforcement efforts. They require destroying firearm purchase data, prohibit the dissemination of specific gun trace data, and forbid the Alcohol, Tobacco, and Firearms (ATF) from establishing gun dealer requirements to submit inventories to law enforcement. Reconciliation of inventories is a key tool for detecting illicit arms sales.

Ban the sale of assault weapons, large magazines (10 rounds maximum per magazine), and trigger activators (bump stocks). Use the Assault Weapons Ban of 2023 (H.R. 698) as the foundation of this portion of the bill, effectively grandfathering in all existing assault weapons but banning the sale or transfer of the same. Add large magazine and bump stock prohibitions and implement a voluntary buyback program. This portion of the law will surely be tested under the Heller precedent. Are semiautomatics "in common use at the time," which would preclude a wholesale ban? Or would this be "a more nuanced approach" that Scalia's opinion referenced in cases of "**unprecedented societal concerns or dramatic technological changes?**" Each element of the law would stand alone, so a subsequent defeat of the assault weapons ban component of the law would not overturn the whole law.

Ammunition accountability. Incorporate 2023's Ammunition Modernization and Monitoring Oversight Act (AMMO Act) S.3223 as the foundation of this component of the bill. The proposal restricts bulk sales of ammunition to 1,000 rounds per five-day period, mandates that sellers hold federal firearm licenses (FFL), and requires the same background checks as firearms. Law-abiding gun owners already in the background check system would obtain instant approval for ammunition purchases.

I would add ammunition serialization to the bill; all ammunition packages will have a unique serial number, and all the rounds within the package will have the serial number marked on the base of the round and the cartridge case. This portion of the bill would be effective two years after the legislation's enactment, giving manufacturers and dealers time to prepare. Each sale would be reported to the gun owners, guns, and ammunition database.

Though liability insurance will be required for firearm purchases, ammunition sales would not face the same requirement. Though the gun lobby will feverishly complain that ammunition accountability requires yet-to-be-obtained technology to introduce at scale, it is common technology. Our pharmaceuticals are commonly coded, and you will find lot numbers on the bottles of over-the-counter medication.

Serialized manufacturing and logistics are here. The gun lobby has worked hard to prohibit proven technological requirements and to shame manufacturers that might offer the latest technology. In addition to keeping insurance rates down, serializing ammunition will provide law enforcement with tools to prosecute the criminal use of firearms. This is nothing that should alarm law-abiding gun owners. The opposition to firearm technology has been the fear of a slippery slope and general contempt of government regulation. Once these laws are enacted and in common practice, the paranoia around firearm regulation should gradually recede.

Incent smart gun technology. Smart guns, also known as personalized guns, are "smart" in that they are only able to be used by the registered owner(s). While the technology is not novel, it is not mature or necessarily reliable as yet. The current technology uses fingerprints or other biometric sensors to confirm the user's identity. RFID chips are another smart gun tool that requires a corresponding wearable token in close proximity to the firearm to operate. Liability insurance rates for such weapons would be extraordinarily cheap, as their accidental use by children or subsequent criminal use by thieves is prevented by smart technology. Parents would presumably appreciate the safety features of the technology and become early adopters once the technology is ready.

I propose that the ATF draft smart gun performance standards and testing protocols pursuant to achieving commercial viability. Federal funds will be used to voluntarily test weapons in training programs within the armed services and federal, state, and local law enforcement agencies. When and if specific smart gun models meet the drafted performance standards, they will be federally approved for sale. In such events, federal funds can be used to support bulk purchases for use in the armed services and to subsidize sales to state and local law enforcement for the same. This will incentivize the industry to develop smart weapons and then manufacture them at scale. America remains the most innovative nation in the world—this is a great opportunity to put our skills to work in solving a uniquely American problem.

It's important to note that none of the above gun safety laws would call for the confiscation of any currently legal firearms. There will be no "gun grabbing." One of the benefits of going big with legislation is that it will put to rest the paranoid fears that some gun owners feel toward their government. Right now, it represents an irrational fear of the unknown. Once our gun laws are more consistent with our peers in Canada and Europe, while (of course) subject to the 2nd Amendment, law-abiding gun owners will realize there is nothing to fear. They will ultimately feel as secure as their cultural peers in the Western world. Criminals and terrorist groups will be frustrated by these laws, as guns will be harder to obtain illegally, and law enforcement will have more tools to serve and protect the public.

EXPAND AND REORGANIZE THE JUDICIARY

Federal judgeships have not been meaningfully expanded since 1990, yet our population grew 33% from 1990 to 2020. In 2017, Steven Calabresi and Shams Hirji published a proposed judgeship bill that would expand the judgeships by 261 seats (61 circuits and 200 districts).[20] They also recommend replacing 158 administrative law judge positions with Article III Administrative Law judgeships. I recommend that Congress authorize and fill all the Calabresi/Hirji recommended positions early in the new Congress.

Mr. Calabresi is a longstanding co-chair of the Federalist Society board of directors, sharing the position with Leonard Leo. Messrs. Leo and Calabresi have successfully engineered the packing of our Supreme Court, playing a key role in the selection of all three of Donald Trump's picks as well as preventing Senate consideration of Merrick Garland. They created the court candidate list from which Trump campaigned. They helped organize the social network that, among other things, appears intended to keep conservative justices in line. They do not want to see Republican appointees moderate or move to the left, as they believe happened with David Souter, John Paul Stevens, Sandra Day O'Connor, and Anthony Kennedy, among others.

In the author's opinion, the largesse of Federalist Society-related donors to the Republican-nominated Supreme Court justices is intended to buy and retain influence. The extravagant vacations, sweetheart real estate deals, and forgiven motorcoach loans are intended primarily to keep the justices in the far-right philosophical fold. Members of the court are receiving favors of significant value as well as an entree into the donor's wealthy social circles. While the seats are lifetime appointments, the extraordinary holidays, gifts, and newfound friendships can go away if a justice is perceived to have forgotten how they got there or where they came from. The justices are human and, as we have recently learned, do not feel particularly constrained by ethics or a code of conduct that would prevent corruption, donor influence, or the appearance thereof.

Calabresi and Hirji made many compelling arguments for expanding the judgeships, including the significant increases in workloads and the shortcuts that the courts are now taking apparently in response to the short staffing, which they described as a "crisis in volume." In fact, they wrote that the optimum number of circuit court positions, excluding the Federal Circuit, should be at least doubled and "more likely between 2.5x and 3.0x the current number." They based this on the Judicial Conference of the United States staffing model and participation rates.

Again, using the Judicial Conference's staffing model, Calabresi and Hirji found a deficit of 185 judgeships at the district court level. Because they felt that it would not be politically possible to add the 352–519 circuit and district court positions called for by staffing models in addition to taking the 158 ALJs to Article III judgeships, they proposed a lesser, politically tenable number. Their formula matched the greatest expansion of the courts, which was under the Omnibus Judgeship Act of 1978. It expanded the circuit court positions by 36.1% and the district court judgeships by 29.7%, which is how they came to additions of 61 and 200, respectively. They advocated 15 more district court seats than the staffing model supported, but that was offset by the 106–273 seat shortfall in the circuit courts. I recommend matching their restraint, which increases the judgeships by roughly the same amount as our population growth since the last major expansion. Of course, I would also add the 158 current ALJ positions to Article III judgeships.

I would also reorganize the appellate courts, folding the DC Circuit into the Federal Circuit for matters concerning the federal district (the vast majority of cases) and the 4th Circuit for matters concerning the new state. I would then form two new circuits: one in Seattle for the northern states of the 9th Circuit and another in Orlando to take pressure off the 4th, 6th, and 11th Circuits. The 9th Circuit currently serves 67 million, and four other fast-growing districts serve at least 30 million. These changes would leave the 9th Circuit with 44 million and only one other—the 5th Circuit—with over 30 million.

The largest circuit would represent 13% of the nation rather than 20% at present, and all others, save for the 5th, would represent less than 10% of our population. The 13 circuits would mirror the new number of Supreme Court judgeships, with one supervising justice per circuit and the Chief Justice also overseeing the Federal Circuit.

When the Democratic Congress adopts the recommendations of the Federalist Society co-chair proposal as a whole, Republicans can hardly complain. It was their idea! Adding only 61 circuit judgeships shows restraint when such august lights opine that the number should really be between 167 and 334. Matching the recommended additions across the board provides political cover.

Republicans, of course, will still find a way to complain. Though they will effectively be disarmed by the Democratic majorities, their political arguments are defeated by Calabresi and Hirji. While Republican officeholders can argue that they didn't expand the courts in 2017 as recommended, that is only because they couldn't. Such legislation currently requires 60 votes in the Senate. It is only after the filibuster has been eliminated that such legislation can be passed.

At the beginning of the 115th Congress in 2017, the Republicans controlled 53 seats in the Senate—three more than they needed to end the filibuster. Mitch McConnell would have loved to send the anachronistic rule packing, but he did not have the votes. Just as Kyrsten Sinema and Joe Manchin prevented the Democrats from such control in 2021, John McCain, Susan Collins, Lisa Murkowski, Jeff Flake, and Bob Corker reputedly objected in 2017.

By varying degrees, none of those Republicans were particularly anxious to grease the skids for Donald Trump. The filibuster will be headed to the dustbin of history should either party sweep the 2024 election. Frankly, that will also signal an expansion of the judiciary as we are objectively in need of more capacity.

US Courts of Appeals Proposed Circuit Composition							1 of 2
Circuit	AJ*	PJ**	±	2000 Census Population	%	Authorized per judge	Proposed per judge
1st - Boston							
Maine				1,362,359			
Massachusetts				7,029,917			
New Hampshire				1,377,529			
Puerto Rico				3,285,874			
Rhode Island				1,097,379			
Total	6	6	0	14,153,058	4%	2,358,843	2,358,843
2nd - New York							
Connecticut				3,605,944			
New York				20,201,249			
Vermont				643,077			
Total	13	16	3	24,450,270	7%	1,880,790	1,528,142
3rd - Philadelphia							
Delaware				989,948			
New Jersey				9,288,994			
Pennsylvania				13,002,700			
Virgin Islands				87,146			
Total	14	14	0	23,368,788	7%	1,669,199	1,669,199
4th - Richmond							
Douglass				689,545			
Maryland				6,177,224			
North Carolina				10,439,388			
Virginia				8,631,393			
West Virginia				1,793,716			
Total	12	24	12	27,731,266	8%	2,310,939	1,155,469
5th - New Orleans							
Louisiana				4,657,757			
Oklahoma				3,959,353			
Texas				29,145,505			
Total	16	27	11	37,762,615	11%	2,360,163	1,398,615
6th - Cincinnati							
Kentucky				4,505,836			
Michigan				10,077,331			
Ohio				11,799,448			
Total	13	15	2	26,382,615	8%	2,029,432	1,758,841
7th - Chicago							
Illinois				12,812,508			
Indiana				6,785,528			
Wisconsin				5,893,718			
Total	11	13	2	25,491,754	8%	2,317,432	1,960,904
8th - St Louis							
Arkansas				3,011,524			
Iowa				3,190,369			
Minnesota				5,706,494			
Missouri				6,154,913			
Nebraska				1,961,504			
North Dakota				779,094			
South Dakota				886,667			
Total	11	14	3	21,690,565	6%	1,971,870	1,549,326

US Courts of Appeals Proposed Circuit Composition

Circuit	AJ*	PJ**	±	2000 Census Population	%	Authorized per judge	Proposed per judge
9th - San Francisco							
California				39,538,223			
Guam				153,836			
Hawaii				1,455,271			
Nevada				3,104,614			
NMI				47,329			
Total	18	25	7	44,299,273	13%	2,461,071	1,771,971
10th - Denver							
Arizona				7,151,502			
Colorado				5,773,714			
Kansas				2,937,880			
New Mexico				2,117,522			
Utah				3,271,616			
Wyoming				576,851			
Total	13	13	0	21,829,085	7%	1,679,160	1,679,160
11th - Atlanta							
Georgia				10,711,908			
South Carolina				5,118,425			
Tennessee				6,910,840			
Total	10	17	7	22,741,173	7%	2,274,117	1,337,716
12th - Seattle							
Alaska				733,391			
Idaho				1,839,106			
Montana				1,084,225			
Oregon				4,237,256			
Washington				7,705,281			
Total	8	11	3	15,599,259	5%	1,949,907	1,418,114
13th - Orlando							
Alabama				5,024,279			
Florida				21,538,187			
Mississippi				2,961,279			
Total	11	22	11	29,523,745	9%	2,683,977	1,341,988
Total	156	217	61	335,023,466	100%	2,147,586	1,543,887
Federal - DC							
District of Columbia	11	11	0				
Other Federal	12	12	0				
Total	179	240	61				

*. AJ = Authorized Judges - the number of currently authorized judgeships as reorganzed
** PJ = Proposed Judges - the number of proposed judgeships as reorganized

IMPLEMENT A REVENUE NEUTRAL CARBON TAX AND DIVIDEND PROGRAM

The next Congress will be too busy to engage in wholesale tax reform. The subsequent Congress will be able to address our Rube Goldberg tax code when they address our debt and deficits, a festering problem that should come to the fore sooner rather than later.

Meanwhile, the Democrats will have an opportunity to fight climate change and speed up the conversion to green energy by way of a revenue-neutral carbon tax. In order to fully refund all the revenues generated by the carbon tax, I propose that we eliminate the carried interest tax loophole to fund the costs of the carbon tax administration.

Add a revenue-neutral carbon tax of $100 per metric ton. This may be a better policy than politics, as it would increase the cost of dirty energy across the board. Gas at the pump would go up about $1.14/gallon.[21] Take the funds received and rebate them quarterly to every American citizen, with full shares to adults and half shares for minors paid to their parents or legal guardians. This would refund approximately $1,200 per individual citizen per year, with about $600 for each minor dependent. A carbon tax is an excise tax, which is typically regressive. However, the broad rebates will more than offset the impact on low-income consumers.

While Americans hate paying higher prices at the pump and on monthly utility bills, both are controllable. Thermostats can be adjusted in the short term, and home sizes can be rationalized over time. Trips can be curtailed now while an electric vehicle (EV) or hybrid becomes a higher consideration in future vehicle purchases. Efficient consumers will effectively be rewarded with dividends at the expense of those who do not prioritize a lifestyle that reduces greenhouse gas emissions. This alone will make tremendous progress in combatting climate change at no cost to the Treasury.

This method is supported by Arthur Laffer, a libertarian economist who is famous for his Reagan-era supply-side napkin chart. It is also supported by those on the left who are most concerned with the catastrophic consequences of climate change. While there is no silver bullet for combatting greenhouse gases, this policy comes closest to that description.

The carbon tax should be as simple and easy to administer as possible by being taxed upstream at the production and importation of carbon, 84% of which is in the energy industry. The tax and rebates should take effect as soon as practicable, perhaps as early as January 1, 2026, depending on when the bill is passed. There will be no phase-in as the tax will take full effect and thus modify consumers' behavior as soon as possible. There will be no scheduled increases in the tax, as those appear to be the least popular politically where a carbon tax has been implemented. A per metric ton tax of $100 is meaningful and should accomplish its objectives. Consumers and producers alike will be able to adapt to the tax and plan on a known quantity.

Border tax adjustments (BTAs) would be incorporated into the law, so that leakage is not suffered as producers relocate to areas without carbon taxes, costing American jobs. World Trade Organization (WTO) and General Agreement on Tariffs and Trade (GATT) rules allow taxes and credits at the border, essentially allowing for carbon taxes to be credited on exports and applied to imports (with credits for carbon taxes already paid).

In order to fully refund all of the receipts of the carbon tax, funds must be found to pay for the administration of the program. I propose that we remove the carried interest tax break loophole that exclusively benefits venture capitalists. Use the Carried Interest Fairness Act of 2024 (S.4123) as a model. The carried interest loophole is a feature of the tax code that allows wealthy venture capitalists (VCs) to pay the lower capital gains tax rate on income that is earned through the sweat of their brow, on which everyone else pays ordinary income taxes. Going forward, the capital gains tax rate will only apply to income earned on capital—the original rationale for a discounted capital gains tax rate.

VCs play a wonderful role in our system, but they will need to pay ordinary income tax on their earnings like everyone else. This is a loophole that has survived all previous reform attempts as Wall Street contributes a great deal to the war chests of both political parties. Kyrsten Sinema reputedly insisted the favored treatment remain in exchange for her vote on the Inflation Reduction Act. Estimates indicate that eliminating the loophole will raise $6.5 billion in revenue over the next decade, which should be more than needed to run the program.[22] Incremental receipts from closing the loophole would be used exclusively to pay for the administration of the carbon tax with any surplus funds applied to the carbon tax rebates.

A carbon tax has been on the Democratic wish list for most of three decades, but it has failed due to the 60-vote threshold of the filibuster and the power of the dirty energy lobby. Democratic senators in key positions, such as Joe Manchin of West Virginia and John Breaux of Louisiana, have prevented a carbon tax from crossing the finish line. In fairness, they were representing the wishes of their voters in coal, gas, and oil country. Gathering a majority in Congress can be difficult if Republicans and energy state Democrats are all no votes. Next year could provide a window of opportunity for Democrats to enact the law while they control the White House and both houses of Congress. If they can't do it then, I don't see it happening in the foreseeable future.

EXPAND THE HOUSE OF REPRESENTATIVES

My proposal for expanding the People's House is ambitious. Passage of this proposal in 2025 would go a long way toward marginalizing big money, enhancing representation, and smoothing the relative power of the states in the Electoral College.

I propose materially increasing the number of seats in the House of Representatives effective with the 2026 federal election and the 120th Congress. Current congressional districts serve about 760,000 residents. House membership has effectively been frozen at 435 seats since 1912 when districts averaged about 212,000 residents—a much more manageable number than the status quo. If we use the 212,000 as our denominator, that brings us to 1,562 seats. We would simply take the 2020 census by state, divide by 212,000, and round to the nearest whole number. California would have 187 seats by virtue of its population. Our four smallest states would have three each. This would, as noted, also influence the Electoral College. While there is no magic number, the 212,000 suggestion ties representation to the time at which the seat count was frozen.

Physically, the U.S. Capitol can be expanded to seat 1,725 members.[23] During renovations, the body can meet in the National Statuary Hall—the House's chamber in the nineteenth century. Office space for additional members can be acquired. There are no practical impediments to significant enlargement.

Smaller district sizes frustrate the interests of big money

as they are more compact and allow for existing local leadership to rise to the position. Popular, well-known mayors, council members, school board members, business and labor leaders would rise to the fore. The smaller, human-level representation of 1912 would weaken the hand of political consultants brought in to increase the name ID of otherwise unknown candidates who do not necessarily have a record of accomplishment within the community. The hand of authenticity would be strengthened.

Governance should improve as members won't need to serve on multiple congressional committees. There are currently over 130 standing committees, non-standing committees, and subcommittees. There are over 450 congressional caucus groups —more than there are members of the body. Representatives will be able to dedicate more time to problem-solving on a committee or subcommittee. Committees will work more efficiently as fewer schedules will be conflicted. Constituent service should also improve as the members and their offices will have fewer people to serve.

The implications for the Electoral College are meaningful. While I do not see the anachronistic institution going away in the foreseeable future, its unintended consequences can be reduced. Currently, a Wyoming voter has 3.8 times the impact of a California voter in the Electoral College—a rather spectacular delta in the high-stakes matter of choosing a president.[24] Increasing House membership to 1,562 would increase the Electoral College to 1,665, including 3 seats for the federal district under the 23rd Amendment, until repealed, which would reduce the ratio to 1.8. That is still too high for my tastes, but it's a marked improvement over the status quo.

Such a protocol would have changed the Electoral College outcome in 2000, with Al Gore comfortably winning. It would not have changed the outcome in 2016, the only other such "popular vote loser wins" scenario in the last century.

With only 435 seats serving a population of 331 million, we also have a greater discrepancy in district sizes due to simple math. Presently, Delaware has one statewide congressional district with 989,948 residents, while Montana has two congressional districts, each with 542,113 at the time of redistricting. Thus, Montanans have 1.82 times the representation in the House as do Delawareans. There is nothing corrupt about it. Rather, it shows the difficulty in providing approximately equal representation in a 435-member body whose role is proportional representation in a very large country. The 212,000 proposal brings the maximum discrepancy to 1.27—a huge ratio reduction—as Wyoming will average 192,284 per seat while Alaska will average 244,464. Both states will have three congressional districts.

Some quarters will complain that there isn't enough time to redistrict 18 months prior to the next election. However, legislatures are always in charge of redistricting after every census. Should this reform be executed during the first three months of the new congressional term, legislatures will have nine months to redistrict during 2025, which isn't even a hard deadline. Pursuant to judicial rulings, several states changed maps in 2024 for the November 2024 federal election. The scope of redistricting will be modest in that the state legislative districts will not need to be redrawn as in standard post-census reapportionment. They will only need to draw a new map for U.S. House districts.

Expanding the House into 1,562 districts effective for the 2026 election also has political advantages. It will require redistricting, which legislatures elected in 2024 will oversee. This book anticipates a Democratic sweep this November, and the legislative elections should reflect the favorable results. Furthermore, the redistricting would take place under the rules of the 2025 Voting Rights Act, which includes anti-gerrymandering components and other improvements to the system.

It's been said that Congress would not want to expand the House because members do not want their positions diluted. For the vast majority, their seats are relatively safe, and as successful politicians, they know their district. Why would they want to jeopardize their seat to become merely one of 1,562 in a brand-new district with significant differences from the status quo? Human nature, it seems, would get in the way.

In fact, human nature may assist in the endeavor. Seasoned politicians will pick the district that fits them the best. Since seats will be expanding 3.6 times, the House member should pick the best district from three or four available. They should find a spot that most closely corresponds to their worldview and will require fewer political calculations when taking positions. Authenticity will again be fostered by the creation of the new districts.

When one party sweeps in a presidential election year, there tends to be a reversion to the mean in the next election. In the 1994 election—the first after President Clinton's resounding victory—Democrats lost 54 seats in the House and 8 in the Senate. Clinton's party had taken tough votes to raise taxes (leading to budget surpluses four years later) and restrict assault rifle sales. There was a conservative backlash to the administration's "Don't ask, don't tell" policy allowing homosexuals to serve in the military. Clinton's failed attempt at healthcare reform lifted the spirits of the Republican Party, which, just two years earlier, had been despondent for losing the White House after holding it for 20 of the last 24 years.

Two years after President Obama was elected and both houses were stocked with solid majorities, the Democrats lost 63 seats in the House and 6 in the Senate. The nation was still in the financial crisis, though the U.S. was leading the free world in recovery. Between the wars in Iraq and Afghanistan, the economic displacement of the financial crisis, and the plodding recovery, the electorate was surly.

Donald Trump suffered a similar fate in 2018, losing 41 House seats and handing the gavel back to Nancy Pelosi. Clinton, Obama, and Trump all learned that the out-group is far more passionate than the in-group. Those displaced from power will show up to vote more reliably than those comfortable in their new surroundings.

The reforms advocated in this book are universally and

manifestly good policies, in the humble opinion of the author. That does not mean that the 2026 election will go well. In fact, we know that it will likely be a down year. The question is one of scale: Will the reversion to the mean switch control in one or both of the houses or will we stubbornly hold control due to a solid House margin and favorable Senate map heading into the election?

This question matters to the representatives who will be running for re-election. Current members' ability to shop for the best-fitting district should comfort them. Members holding competitive seats will not have to decide between voting for good policy and keeping their jobs. A safer seat will likely be available in '26.

They will have the political freedom to do the right thing. They will also have seniority in the next Congress. While half of the current members are in the lower half of seniority, they will all be in roughly the top quarter of the next. They will have a better opportunity to find a committee to serve that addresses their top priorities.

While the new House configuration offers myriad intrinsic benefits, it will also allow for the most consequential Congress in history. Members will vote their conscience and address a long list of Democratic priorities that had been prevented by the filibuster.

This is important, as the Democrats should proceed with the knowledge that they have a fleeting two-year opportunity. They should assume that they will lose control of the House in 2026, which history tells us is a better-than-even bet. However, the individual members do not need to lose their seats for doing the right thing.

CREATE SEVEN CALIFORNIAS

The U.S. Senate is less representative than it has ever been. California has 68 times the population of Wyoming, yet they receive the same membership in the upper body. The Golden State is our most populous, with nearly 40 million residents, yet it enjoys the same representation as Wyoming—population 576,851 in the 2020 census—in the Senate. That's not a typo—Californians receive less than 2% of the representation in our upper body as do the residents of our smallest state. This is a significant increase in the ratio that the founders established. In 1790, the largest state, Virginia, had 13 times the population of the smallest state, Delaware.

According to a *Washington Post* analysis, the Republican Party has controlled the Senate roughly half the time in the last 25 years, but they never represented a majority of the nation during that time.[25] In fact, right now, the Democrats control the Senate with 51 seats while representing 58.6% of the U.S. population, including Washington, DC.

If the 57 state proposals—statehood for DC and splitting California into seven states—were implemented in the current Congress, they would increase Democratic control of the Senate from 51/49 to 65/49. That means that the Republicans would hold 43% of seats, which is still 1.6 points more than the red state population. The 57%–43% split would more closely represent the country.

In the event that neither presidential candidate receives a majority of Electoral College votes, the House of Representatives will elect the President, while the Senate will elect the Vice President. However, it isn't a simple vote of House members. Each state delegation has one vote, and Republicans currently control 26 delegations to the Democrats 22. There are two tied delegations (Minnesota and North Carolina). This is what the Trump insurrection was all about after the 2020 election. The goal was to have Pence throw out the Electoral College votes, thus delivering the decision from the people to the House of Representatives with a majority of Republican-controlled delegations.

The 57-state proposals would take the state delegation count to 29 Democratic, 26 Republican, and two tied. Again, this would correspond more closely to the will of the people and remove another tool of minority rule.

While the Republicans control the least populous states, they also control the whitest. The states with the largest populations are, with exceptions, also the most diverse. 34% of California is non-Hispanic White. Wyoming is 83% in the same category. Montana and the two Dakotas are roughly the same demographically as Wyoming.

The Washington Post study found that non-Hispanic Whites are overrepresented by 14% in the Senate—a very large delta. Whites make up 46% of the largest five states but 78% of the five smallest states. Thus, Black and Brown interests are structurally diluted in the Senate today, and these groups are already subject to disadvantages in generational wealth, income, and access to healthcare, among other things. These are the last folks who should have an electoral system stacked against them.

Minority rule—Republican advantages—also prevent popular policies from being enacted, which leads to frustration of the electorate. When issues that 80% of the people support cannot even get a vote in the Senate, the system is broken. This is not sustainable. Minority rule created the current 6 to 3 super-majority in the Supreme Court when they have not held a popular majority in decades. The Republicans have lost the popular vote for president in seven of the last eight presidential elections, yet they confirmed five of the six conservative Supreme Court justices in that same time period.

The Senate confirms presidential appointments—key government officials who run the various agencies and departments that make our country go. The body confirms judges, generals, and cabinet members, among others. Senate appointments need to roughly reflect the will of the people rather than being a bulwark for minority rule. Trump's 2017 tax cut package that cut corporate taxes and added $2 trillion to the national debt was approved by a narrow majority—51 votes in the Senate, representing only 44% of the population. Again, this situation is not fair, democratic, or sustainable.

Proposals to carve up the Golden State have been common since its admission to the union in 1850. It is time for California to become a region rather than a single state, and this can be accomplished in the next Congress if Democrats obtain control. While we have seen proposals for splits of two states to six, my proposal is for seven states, all of which will be initially blue. This is a product of California's electorate, not gerrymandering.

In fact, my proposal leaves every county intact save for Los Angeles County, which would see portions go to Orange California (Orange County and the eastern Gateway Cities) and East California (San Bernardino, Riverside, and Imperial counties, along with the Pomona Valley). The balance of Los Angeles County would be West California, San Diego County would be California Sur, and the five Bay Area counties would comprise California Bays. Five coastal counties from Ventura to Santa Cruz plus San Benito and Kern counties would become Coastal California, and the balance would be Alta California, with its capital in Sacramento. The latter state would contain roughly half the land mass of the current state. Unlike most of the previous 21st-century proposals, the proposed new states share existing communities of interest and are cohesive and constructed logically.

The seven new states are balanced in size, with four larger

than the national median and three smaller. None are in the top 10 states in population or the bottom 20. All seven have large economies, robust infrastructure, and the political cohesion that one would expect from a state. In fact, in their own ways, each would become a model of sorts.

Texas, Florida, and New York may want to divide in the future, and California could give them a meaningful road map. If Texas and Florida were divided into five and three states, respectively, I suspect that we would see many purple and blue states in addition to red. New York would probably create a deep blue state and a couple of purple states if it divided into three.

It has been suggested that dividing California would take years and necessarily face multiple lawsuits. Such dysfunction can be avoided by enabling legislation that would necessarily be passed by Congress and the California legislature. The split would be enacted by way of a statute, thus requiring only a simple majority of the Assembly and Senate along with the governor's signature. No election is required, and it need not be time-consuming.

The enabling legislation would allocate operating cash and general obligation bonds to the states based on the 2020 census population. Lease-revenue bonds and traditional revenue bonds would be the responsibility of the states in which the related facilities are located. Pension funds and obligations incurred to date would be allocated by the census population. Ownership of facilities would transfer to the state in which they are located.

Multistate compacts would be created to address issues —primarily transportation and natural resources—that would maintain current rights and responsibilities and prevent disruption to services. Such compacts are commonly employed throughout the country. Compacts may be used to address the transition, particularly in the education and corrections departments, among others. Initially, reciprocity would be established in areas such as state licensure and tuition status for college students. California is currently a party to 33 interstate compacts, going back to 1922 (the Colorado River Compact).

The existing state statutes and constitution would be the same for each of the new states, and no new conventions would be required. The initial legislatures would be comprised of members representing districts within the new state boundaries. Districts that overlap would be allocated to the state in which most residents reside, and rump districts would be allocated to adjacent districts within the new state.

Current statewide office holders would retain their positions, self-selecting the respective state for the balance of their terms, provided that they won their last elections within the boundaries of the new state and reside in the same. The initial legislatures would appoint the open positions of the statewide offices (governor, lieutenant governor, attorney general, secretary of state, treasurer, controller, superintendent of public instruction, and insurance commissioner) of the new states to serve until the positions are filled in the 2026 general election.

The initial legislatures would redistrict their respective 80 Assembly and 40 Senate seats to be filled in the 2026 election. As State Senate seat terms are four years and half the Senate is elected every other year, State Senators with terms ending in 2028 would retain their seats, self-selecting the new district provided that they won within the new district boundaries in the last election and reside in the same. If two such senators both selected the same new district, the senator with the most votes in the last election within the new district would prevail.

Since nearly 40 million Californians are currently represented by only 120 legislators over both houses, the residents of the seven states will enjoy significantly more representation with 120 legislators in each of the states. The California Split states range in size from 3.2 million to 8.5 million, so voters will receive at least 4.6 times the representation as present and up to 12.4 times the current ratio. Current state Senate districts comprise nearly a million residents, which stretches one state legislator extraordinarily thin. Further, legislators need to assiduously court big money to fund campaigns that have to reach so many voters. The largest state Senate districts will now serve about 214,000—a much more human scale wherein many local activists will already be known to the electorate and will not have to cater to lobbyists to fund their campaigns.

The current State Supreme Court would seed the new State Supreme Courts, with each member becoming the chief justice of each respective court. The superior and appellate courts would be allocated geographically. The open seats on the courts would be filled under the established rules of governor appointment subject to the approval of the state's newly populated Commissions on Judicial Nominees for Evaluation and the Commissions on Judicial Appointments.

The existing congressional districts would remain in place, with the new legislatures allocating rump territory to adjacent districts until the next reapportionment. They would retain the right to draw up new districts, though that may be a heavy lift with all the other changes afoot.

The two current senators would self-select the new state that they would represent for the balance of their term provided that they won within their new state boundaries in the last election and reside in the same. It is safe to assume that Alex Padilla and Adam Schiff, subject to victory in the 2024 election, would both select West California and retain their seats on that basis.

The initial legislatures would appoint the open seats. The enabling legislation would identify which two Senate classes each state would hold. The 2026 election would elect the Class 2 member (term ends 2033), if any. If the state does not hold a Class 2 position, the Class 1 seat (term ends 2031) would be subject to election in 2026. The Class 3 seat (term ends 2035) would be subject to election in 2028. If the state does not have a Class 3 seat, the Class 1 seat would be elected in 2028 to serve until 2031. This protocol would establish that all seven states would have a senatorial election in 2026 and again in 2028 so that no appointed Senators would serve more than three years without facing the voters.

Properly drafted enabling legislation will grease the skids for a successful transition to seven states. With the 2024 elected legislature drafting the rules of the road, every interest will have a seat at the table. It need not be an acrimonious process, and all seven states should win. It is not a zero-sum game. Californians will have significantly more representation in their new statehouses, and more positions of impact will be filled. Only one governor and two senators for 40 million people isn't merely a paltry representation, but it also doesn't provide a sufficient number of positions for effective, popular, and enterprising people to contribute. The California region will offer the nation far more leaders than it is able to presently. Californians will have substantially more representation at the state and federal levels than they currently enjoy.

The new states will craft discrete legislation, and the respective electorates will bring forth their own unique initiatives. Sharing the existing statutes initially will merely be a starting point. In time, the various states will have laws, tax rates, and policy priorities tailored to the needs of their constituents.

Ultimately, East California will not have the same tax rates and spending programs as California Bays. Neither will Alta California and West California. Nor should they. Yet they will all share the benefits of natural resources, transportation systems, and other regional priorities by way of compacts. The California region will blossom with the flexibility brought by the seven states as proposed.

Alta California will have an 8.5 million population covering north and central California, less the Bay Area and the coastal counties south of the same. It includes urban, suburban, exurban, and rural areas. Alta California will be the twelfth largest state by population, just below Virginia and larger than West California and Washington state. Sacramento will be the capital, with UC Davis as the flagship school and UC Merced a close second. It will be a comfortably blue state, having voted Democratic by 10–14 points in each of the last four presidential elections. The economy is diversified, with technology, healthcare, agriculture, manufacturing, and services all well-represented.

The ratio of residents to state Assembly members will be 1/107,228 and the Senate 1/214,456—nearly five times more representation in both houses than presently enjoy. This will reduce the impact of money in elections, as well-known members of the community will emerge without having to spend money to establish name identification. They will not need to be introduced to the community as would someone seeking to represent a million people. City council and school board members could naturally leap to the Assembly. Business leaders, community activists, and lifelong residents will have an opportunity to be elected by their neighbors.

California Bays, named after the San Francisco and San Pablo Bays – the Bay Area – will be the bluest of the seven new states, having voted against Trump nearly four to one in the last two elections. Having just lost the Raiders and soon the A's, Oakland will gain newfound relevance as the new state's capital. UC Berkley will be the flagship school, followed by UC San Francisco. The five counties comprising the state are urban and suburban. Technology is the primary industry as the Bay Area is the tech capital of the world.

With a population of 6.4 million, it will be the 19th largest state in the union, just smaller than Indiana and narrowly larger than Missouri. The ratio of residents to Assembly members is 1/80,287—six times the current representation.

California Sur—currently San Diego County—will be a very efficient state as it will remove a layer of government, combining county responsibilities with the state. Sur will be reliably blue, as it voted Democratic by over 20 points in the last two presidential elections. It has been on a leftward trajectory over the last 20 years, as it voted for Bush by six points in 2004, Obama by 10 points in 2008, and Joe Biden by 14 points in 2020.

California Sur will be the second smallest state of the seven, with 3.3 million residents, 27% below the median state size. It will be just larger than Coastal California and Utah while smaller than Connecticut. The economy is diverse, with a significant defense and military presence, as well as manufacturing, agriculture, and tourism. Sur is a border state with Tijuana just past the southern border.

Coastal California will have a population of 3.2 million, the smallest of the seven, just smaller than California Sur and narrowly larger than Iowa. The capital will be in San Luis Obispo, and residents will enjoy a ratio of 1/40,723 in the Assembly, half that in the Senate, which is twelve times the current representation. The flagship school is UC Santa Barbara.

The new state's diversified economy includes aerospace, defense, tourism, agriculture, and healthcare. Politically, it will be reliably blue, as it voted Democratic in every presidential election in the century, with Biden receiving more than 60% of the vote in 2020.

East California contains the Inland Empire of Riverside and San Bernardino counties, along with Imperial County and the Pomona Valley sliver of Los Angeles County. The population is 5.1 million, 13% more than the median state size, just smaller than Alabama and larger than Louisiana.

Riverside will be the state capital, and UC Riverside will be the flagship school. The three counties voted Democratic by a 10-point margin in the last two presidential elections and by about five points in the preceding two elections.

The economy features transportation, warehousing, and logistics, with agriculture still present but declining in relative terms. Education, healthcare, manufacturing, and tourism round out the largest contributors.

Orange California contains the eponymous county plus the eastern Gateway Cities of Los Angeles County, with a population of 4.5 million, right in line with the median state size. Kentucky is slightly larger, and Oregon is just smaller. The capitol will be in Santa Ana, the current county seat, and the flagship school will be UC Irvine.

The new state is home to many Fortune 500 firms,

particularly in technology, defense, and aerospace. Healthcare, manufacturing, tourism, and services are the largest employers.

OC should be reliably blue, though that is a recent development. Until Trump was the Republican standard bearer, the county was consistently red. The margins in the last two presidential elections were nine and 10 points, and with the addition of the eastern Gateway Cities, OC should be comfortably blue.

West California is the second largest of the seven new states, with 8.4 million residents. It is essentially LA County, less the eastern Gateway Cities and Pomona Valley. West California will be the thirteenth-largest state, just smaller than Virginia and Alta California while larger than Washington.

The state is the center of the nation's entertainment industry and hosts many Fortune 500 corporate headquarters. The Port of Los Angeles is the ninth largest by volume in the country. The biggest industries are aerospace, defense, biosciences, technology, manufacturing, and healthcare. Like most of the other California states, the economy is diversified.

The county voted Democratic nearly three to one in the last two presidential elections. Los Angeles will be the capital, and UCLA will naturally be the flagship school.

California has seen many proposals for division since statehood. It is logical that a state of 39 million in a nation with a median state population of 4.5 million would need to split to meet the needs of its vast citizenry, create more leadership platforms, and increase representation in the Senate and Electoral College.

I provide a specific map to judge the plan on its merits. The proposed states are rational, cohesive, and easy to implement. Every county but Los Angeles survives intact. I outlined the principles—a road map—for a quick, efficient split that will avoid the mischief-making of a prolonged process. We can begin 2025 with 50 states and end the year with 57 states. In such a scenario, the Senate will have 14 more Democratic seats. This gain will not last forever. Just as Massachusetts frequently elects moderate Republican governors and even a Republican Senator in a special election, the California region will occasionally elect centrist Republicans. But the small state advantage that the GOP has held for decades will be gone. The Democratic fear of a presidential election being decided by the House of Representatives will recede as the state count will be more balanced. For the past 30 years, that would have locked in a Republican victory regardless of the votes at the state or national level. That will no longer hold.

State	Capital	Flagship University	2020 Population*	CD Current	Population per CD	CD Proposed	Population per CD	Senate Classes**
Alta California (AC)	Sacramento	UC Davis	8,578,268	11	779,843	40	214,457	1, 3
Alpine, Amador, Butte, Calaveras, Colusa, Del Norte, El Dorado, Fresno, Glenn, Humboldt, Inyo, Kings, Lake, Lassen, Madera, Marin, Mariposa, Mendocino, Merced, Modoc, Mono, Nevada, Placer, Plumas, Sacramento, San Joaquin, Shasta, Sierra, Siskiyou, Solano, Stanislaus, Sutter, Tehama, Trinity, Tulare, Tuolumne, Yolo, & Yuba counties.								
California Bays (CB)	Oakland	UC Berkley	6,422,946	9	713,661	30	214,098	1, 3
Alameda, Contra Costa, San Francisco, San Mateo, & Santa Clara counties.								
California Sur (CS)	San Diego	UCSD	3,298,634	4	824,659	16	206,165	1, 2
San Diego County.								
Coastal California (CC)	San Luis Obispo	UCSB	3,257,836	4	814,459	15	217,189	1, 2
Kern, Monterey, San Benito, San Luis Obispo, Santa Barbara, Santa Cruz, & Ventura counties.								
East California (EC)	Riverside	UC Riverside	5,089,850	7	727,121	24	212,077	2, 3
Imperial, Riverside, and San Bernardino counties plus Pomona Valley.								
Orange California (OC)	Santa Ana	UC Irvine	4,491,279	6	748,547	21	213,870	2, 3
Orange County plus noted Gateway Cities.								
West California (WC)	Los Angeles	UCLA	8,399,410	11	763,583	40	209,985	1, 3
LA County less noted Gateway Cities & less Pomona Valley.								
Total			**39,538,223**	**52**	**760,350**	**186**	**212,571**	

* 2020 population is per the 2020 Census. EC, OC, and WC are estimates based on the 2020 Census.

** Senate Class 1 takes office in 2025; Class 2 in 2027; Class 3 in 2029.

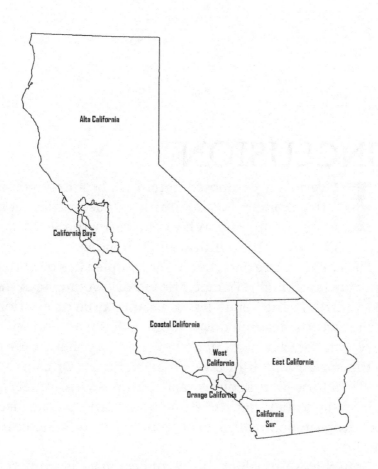

Alta California

California Bays

Coastal California

West California

East California

Orange California

California Sur

CONCLUSION

Everything proposed herein is absolutely possible if the Democrats pick up the House while retaining the Senate and White House in the 2024 general election. Will there be the political will? I hope so.

The conservative entertainment complex has been treating each election as though a Democratic victory would mean the end of the country. To the Republicans, a Kamala Harris election will mean that we are heading down the socialist path and will soon go the way of Venezuela or Cuba (they never cry that we are going down the socialist path of Sweden or Norway). Of course, such alarmist rhetoric is ridiculous, and Europeans routinely laugh when it is suggested that the Democratic Party is socialist. If it were a European political party, it would be viewed as centrist or center-right.

Nonetheless, much of the Republican base is going to freak out with Democrats winning the White House and both houses of Congress. Donald Trump will make matters worse by again claiming a rigged vote, no matter the scale of his loss or the absence of any proof of his claims. We may as well go big, as the MAGA crowd will be apoplectic no matter what we do. There is nothing to be gained by going small or incremental.

They will not be calmed when the Democrats kill the filibuster, expand the Supreme Court, and grant statehood to DC with its implications for the Senate. When the Democrats ensure abortion rights, raise the minimum wage, and enact a new Voting Rights Act in the first 100 days, the GOP will claim the end of the republic is nigh. They are not used to losing and are particularly jealous of their built-in electoral and legislative advantages. They like their privilege, and they won't lose it quietly. But lose it they will, and after a commensurate period of wailing and moaning, they will adjust and adapt to the new reality. Life will go on in these United States and materially improve as we solve problems that have bedeviled us for generations.

The right has won many battles in the 21ˢᵗ century, largely through the courts. They just finished their 49-year project of overturning Roe v. Wade. Their previous majority and now supermajority on the Supreme Court has kept Republican priorities safe across the board concerning abortion rights (Dodds), voting rights (Shelby), and individual rights to firearms (Heller).

They have granted widespread immunity to presidents from criminal prosecution, giving Trump wide latitude should he be reelected and partially protecting him from past crimes. They slow-walked their opinions to the benefit of Trump after rejecting Special Prosecutor Jack Smith's request for expedited review in 2023.

The Supreme Court, of course, acted quickly concerning decisions in the Watergate era and they moved with lightning speed in Bush v. Gore. It is hard to find that *this* court is acting in good faith. Rather, they seem to have their thumb on the scale favoring the man who gave them their 6–3 majority. Alito, Thomas, and Gorsuch have all violated ethics standards with impunity.

As Lord Acton said, "Power tends to corrupt, and absolute power corrupts absolutely." Fortunately, the Supreme Court that the Federalist Society worked for decades to obtain can be gone in one election cycle. They have given us every reason to expand and unpack the court.

This book does not advocate a radical shift in the operations of the Supreme Court, and all the legislative prescriptions herein would be legal and consistent with the Dodds, Shelby, and Heller rulings. Those decisions remain the law of the land—and likely will for the foreseeable future. But the great leap to the right will be over as the court is unpacked and we return to a centrist, consensus-building judiciary like we enjoyed from the Warren, Burger, and even Rehnquist courts. Many issues, especially reproductive rights, can be addressed through legislation in 2025.

Of course, the Democrats will remain busy after the first 100 days, passing comprehensive immigration reform, gun safety laws, and a stiff revenue-neutral carbon tax. All three are issues that animate the MAGA base. That should not scare the good guys away. In fact, getting past these issues may well lead to domestic peace. Actually, solving long-festering problems is good policy and good politics. The right-wing paranoia around guns, in particular, has infected our discourse. It has led to otherwise nice people threatening a civil war. Less nice right-wingers are hoping for a civil war to arrive so that they will be able to go Travis Bickle on Antifa, "libtards," and of course, Democrats. But passing the legislation—eliminating the threat of the same and making the policies tangible—will gradually remove their fears. They will see that no one is showing up to grab their guns. Law-abiding gun owners will find that their lives do not change at all, except they are safer.

When we have immigration reform that genuinely secures the border and provides for internal enforcement, who will suffer? What will they have to fear when they no longer see hordes of immigrants making their way north or camped near the border? When our economy is not thrown into deep recession by the wholesale deportation of millions of workers providing essential labor at a reasonable price, who will complain?

Our education and medical systems will simply continue apace. Who will cry foul as our country becomes richer as doctors, scientists, and engineers fill more spots in an expanded legal immigration system?

We are in an economy that will welcome more legal workers at all levels. The fears that have so carefully been ginned up on Fox News, OANN, and Newmax will melt away once the immigration bill is passed and implemented.

Climate change is a phenomenon accepted by the scientific

community worldwide in countries governed by every system imaginable. The jury is in, and it is alarmed. Yet, the subject remains part of our culture wars. Our MAGA friends love to criticize electric cars, windmills, and green policy in general. They, of course, offer no solution to the crisis and simply deny the problem.

Somehow, guys who barely finished high school feel comfortable arguing atmospheric science with atmospheric scientists holding PhDs. The fact that the government plays a role in solving the problem is a problem for folks who tend to be *anti-gubment* unless it involves personal receipt of federal assistance. Adding a tax that distributes all the receipts directly to citizens removes much of the dissatisfaction found by a simple tax hike. Most Americans accept climate change, the number continues to grow, and a government that is acting to combat greenhouse gas emissions will ultimately be rewarded. Once the tax is in place and bank accounts are seeing direct deposits, much of the opposition will melt away.

I expect the carbon tax to put pressure on the global price of energy when the world's largest energy producer and consumer implements such a policy. The market will recognize the long-term bearish implications for dirty energy demand and respond accordingly. Prices will drop, reducing the impact of the new tax on Americans at Russian, Saudi, and Iranian expense. This is another proposal that will eliminate the boogeyman upon implementation of the policy. Sure, big oil and coal producers will bitterly complain as will like-minded news channels, but most voters will appreciate the purpose of discouraging dirty energy while enjoying the newfound quarterly income.

The expansion and reform of the judiciary will face bitter opposition from the right, but it will be short-lived. We will have simply implemented Federalist Society plans. What were the political consequences of the large judgeship increases in 1978 and 1990? There were none. They simply became facts on the ground. The complaints here will be minor compared to the expansion of the Supreme Court, which hopefully will lead to constitutional changes that will greatly reduce the partisan angst around our justice system.

Expansion of the House of Representatives will likely find friends and enemies on both sides of the aisle. It will not benefit either political party per se. It will frustrate lobbyists and big money that are quite satisfied with the status quo. It will empower grassroots movements, which clearly come in all flavors. It will bring our government much closer to the people.

The Seven Californias proposal would have the greatest impact on the political balance of Congress. Initially, it would mean 12 new Democratic Senators, which would cause much howling and gnashing of teeth on Team Red. However, the new states will not always elect Democrats, and, as we have seen in the Northeast, several may elect Republican governors. Political changes are never static. Today, West Virginia is one of our reddest states. In 1980, it voted for President Carter over Ronald Reagan by a comfortable four and a half points. Just as the South and West have seen the Democrats gain relevance, Republicans have made inroads in the industrial heartland.

The Democrat's blue wall was breached in 2016 and can no longer be viewed as reliable. They are swing states, and neighboring Ohio is downright red. Should the California Split be implemented in 2025 or 2026, the bitter rhetoric should again be short-lived as it simply becomes a fact on the ground. We will more likely hear Republican calls to make similar changes in Florida and Texas, which would not necessarily be a problem.

The actions advocated in this book will greatly upset the MAGA base as they are egged on by Fox News, Newsmax, OANN, and other alarmist outlets. The deck has been stacked in their favor for years, they have come to expect favored treatment, and they deeply resent any threat to their status. They will show up to vote in 2026, and they will be angry—even if our economy is the best in the world, the president has united the West against an authoritarian foe, and we are building more infrastructure than any time in the last 50 years.

They may well win the 2026 elections, and we need to enact

legislation in a two-year window that will fly by. We will be on the clock, and there will be no time to waste.

The success of the proposals herein will be made possible only by the courageous and principled efforts of Democrats and like-minded independents. However, their passage will not be a partisan victory. In fact, many of the proposals intentionally foster cooperation and end our polarization. The filibuster's demise ultimately serves both parties, as what is fair for one is fair for all. Strategies that rely on blocking legislation will give way to political incentives for participation and collaboration.

The expansion of the Supreme Court will neutralize the packing of the McConnell/Trump era and bring about court membership that is more aligned with the American people and mainstream jurisprudential theory. If the proposed constitutional amendment is passed, justices will be seated in an organized and predictable manner. The stakes of each appointment will be significantly reduced, creating fewer moments of high tension and acrimony in the capitol.

The voting rights proposals are all about making the system fairer and more inclusive. Solving immigration, border security, and gun safety—long-festering issues frustrated by the filibuster—will allow Congress to move on to other pressing issues. These plans will help us heal our divided country.

Partisan legislation will not solve the Rube Goldberg tax code, rising national debt, and consequent interest expenses. They are too big. Solutions need to come sooner rather than later and be crafted to last.

Economic strength and political unity are the tools we use to shape our world. Our failure will only aid authoritarians in China, Russia, Iran, and other states that eschew democracy, free markets, free speech, and the rule of law. The proposals herein will build a wonderful foundation for our continued leadership in the world, but first, they must be enacted.

References

[1] Danielle All Gallup, Inc. "Satisfaction With the United States | Gallup Historical Trends." Gallup.com, October 27, 2022. https://news.gallup.com/poll/1669/general-mood-country.aspx.

[2] "U.S. Senate: Cloture Motions," July 28, 2024. https://www.senate.gov/legislative/cloture/clotureCounts.htm.

[3] Balara, Victoria. "Fox News Poll: Voters Favor Gun Limits Over Arming Citizens to Reduce Gun Violence." Fox News, April 27, 2023. https://www.foxnews.com/official-polls/fox-news-poll-voters-favor-gun-limits-arming-citizens-reduce-gun-violence.

[4] Blest, Paul. "Now Neil Gorsuch Has His Own Mystery Money Scandal." *Vice News*, April 25, 2023. https://www.vice.com/en/article/88xnw3/neil-gorsuch-colorado-property-sale-ethics.

[5] Hinkle, Jordan. "Confidence in the Supreme Court Remains Low - AP-NORC." AP-NORC -, July 11, 2024. https://apnorc.org/projects/confidence-in-the-supreme-court-remains-low/.

[6] "General Election 2016 - Certified Results," n.d. https://web.archive.org/web/20180209232929/https://www.dcboe.org/election_info/election_results/v3/2016/November-8-General-Election.

[7] Newkirk, Vann R., II. "The Republican Party Emerges From Decades of Court Supervision." *The Atlantic*, January 10, 2018. https://www.theatlantic.com/politics/archive/2018/01/the-gop-just-received-another-tool-for-suppressing-votes/550052/.

[8] The Nation. "How The 2000 Election in Florida Led to a New Wave of Voter Disenfranchisement | the Nation," August 3, 2015. https://www.thenation.com/article/archive/how-the-2000-election-in-florida-led-to-a-new-wave-of-voter-disenfranchisement/.

[9] Mock, Brentin. "What Effect Will Shuttering Alabama DMV Offices Have on Black Voters?," October 1, 2015. https://www.bloomberg.com/news/articles/2015-10-01/alabama-closes-dmv-offices-a-year-after-voter-id-law-kicks-in.

[10] Harper, Karen Brooks. "Crystal Mason's 5-year Illegal Voting Sentence Is Overturned." *The Texas Tribune*, March 29, 2024. https://www.texastribune.org/2024/03/28/texas-illegal-voting-conviction-crystal-mason/.

[11] OpenSecrets.org, Election Trends, accessed March 14, 2024, https://www.opensecrets.org/elections-overview/election-trends.

[12] Wasserman, David. "2024 CPR House Race Ratings | Cook Political Report." Cook Political Report, n.d. https://www.cookpolitical.com/ratings/house-race-ratings.

[13] Congress.gov website, retrieved on June 15, 2024: https://www.congress.gov/bill/118th-congress/senate-bill/701.

[14] The Center for American Progress website, retrieved June 16, 2024: https://www.americanprogress.org/article/raising-the-minimum-wage-would-be-an-investment-in-growing-the-middle-class/

[15] Economic Policy Institute. "The Productivity–Pay Gap," n.d. https://www.epi.org/productivity-pay-gap/.

[16] Neumark, David, William Wascher, Joseph Sabia, Richard Burkhauser, and Federal Reserve Bank of Chicago. *It Would Result in Job Loss*, n.d. https://www.cato.org/sites/cato.org/files/four_reasons_not_to_raise_the_minimum_wage.pdf.

[17] BDO. "The Counter: Restaurant Industry Scorecard | September 2019," September 13, 2019. https://www.bdo.com/

insights/industries/restaurants/the-counter-restaurant-industry-scorecard-fc98e1caef274fd51f8e822aab50a813.

[18] CONGRESSIONAL BUDGET OFFICE. "COST ESTIMATE." Report, June 18, 2013. https://www.cbo.gov/system/files/113th-congress-2013-2014/costestimate/s744_0.pdf.

[19] Social Security Administration, Office of the Chief Actuary, Jon Baselice, Alice Wade, Michael Morris, Tiffany Bosley, Mark Bye, et al. "Letter to the Honorable Marco Rubio Regarding the Financial Effects of Senate Bill S. 744 on Social Security." Report. *Letter*, June 28, 2013. https://www.ssa.gov/oact/solvency/MRubio_20130627.pdf.

[20] Calabresi, Steven G., Northwestern University Pritzker School of Law, and Shams Hirji. "Proposed Judgeship Bill." Report. *Northwestern University Pritzker School of Law*, November 7, 2017. https://archive.thinkprogress.org/uploads/2017/11/calabresi-court-packing-memo.pdf.

[21] Rajgopal, Shivaram. "Would a $100 per Ton Carbon Tax Get ExxonMobil to Right Its Errant Ways?" *Forbes*, August 9, 2021. https://www.forbes.com/sites/shivaramrajgopal/2021/08/06/would-a-100-per-ton-carbon-tax-get-exxonmobil-to-right-its-errant-ways/?sh=6d16959f635f.

[22] PricewaterhouseCoopers. "President Biden's FY 2025 Budget Again Calls for Corporate and Individual Tax Increases." PwC, n.d. https://www.pwc.com/us/en/services/tax/library/biden-fy2025-budget-calls-again-for-corporate-and-individual-tax-increases.html.

[23] Allen, Danielle "Can the Capitol hold a much bigger House? Yes, here's how it would look," *The Washington Post*, May 2, 2023. https://www.washingtonpost.com/opinions/interactive/2023/capitol-house-representatives-expansion-design/

[24] California has 54 Electoral College votes and a population

of 39,538,223, or one Electoral College vote per 732,189 residents. Wyoming has 3 EC votes with 576,851 population, or 192,284 residents per EC vote. The ratio is 3.8 to 1.0.

[25] Balz, Dan, Clara Ence Morse, Nick Mourtoupalas. "The Hidden Biases at Play in the US Senate," *The Washington Post,* November 17, 2023. https://www.washingtonpost.com/ politics/interactive/2023/us-senate-bias-white-rural-voters/

Made in the USA
Las Vegas, NV
28 September 2024

95904252R00056